Cambridge Elements

Cambridge Elements in International Economics
edited by
Kenneth A. Reinert
George Mason University

HOW THE BRADY PLAN DELIVERED ON DEBT RELIEF

Lessons and Implications

Neil Shenai
International Monetary Fund

Marijn A. Bolhuis
International Monetary Fund

Shaftesbury Road, Cambridge CB2 8EA, United Kingdom

One Liberty Plaza, 20th Floor, New York, NY 10006, USA

477 Williamstown Road, Port Melbourne, VIC 3207, Australia

314–321, 3rd Floor, Plot 3, Splendor Forum, Jasola District Centre, New Delhi – 110025, India

103 Penang Road, #05–06/07, Visioncrest Commercial, Singapore 238467

Cambridge University Press is part of Cambridge University Press & Assessment, a department of the University of Cambridge.

We share the University's mission to contribute to society through the pursuit of education, learning and research at the highest international levels of excellence.

www.cambridge.org
Information on this title: www.cambridge.org/9781009747400

DOI: 10.1017/9781009747417

© Neil Shenai and Marijn A. Bolhuis 2026

This publication is in copyright. Subject to statutory exception and to the provisions of relevant collective licensing agreements, no reproduction of any part may take place without the written permission of Cambridge University Press & Assessment.

When citing this work, please include a reference to the DOI 10.1017/9781009747417

First published 2026

A catalogue record for this publication is available from the British Library

ISBN 978-1-009-74740-0 Hardback
ISBN 978-1-009-74743-1 Paperback
ISSN 2753-9326 (online)
ISSN 2753-9318 (print)

Cambridge University Press & Assessment has no responsibility for the persistence or accuracy of URLs for external or third-party internet websites referred to in this publication and does not guarantee that any content on such websites is, or will remain, accurate or appropriate.

For EU product safety concerns, contact us at Calle de José Abascal, 56, 1°, 28003 Madrid, Spain, or email eugpsr@cambridge.org

How the Brady Plan Delivered on Debt Relief

Lessons and Implications

Cambridge Elements in International Economics

DOI: 10.1017/9781009747417
First published online: January 2026

Neil Shenai
International Monetary Fund

Marijn A. Bolhuis
International Monetary Fund

Author for correspondence: Neil Shenai, nshenai@imf.org

Abstract: In March 1989, US Treasury Secretary Nicholas Brady introduced a plan enabling distressed sovereigns to restructure unsustainable debts through "Brady bonds." Today, growing debt vulnerabilities have prompted calls for a modern Brady Plan to facilitate sovereign debt restructurings. This Element examines the macroeconomic impact of the original Brady Plan by comparing outcomes for ten Brady countries against forty other emerging markets (EMs) and developing economies. It finds that following the first Brady-led restructuring in 1990, participating countries saw reductions in public and external debt burdens, alongside output and productivity growth anchored by strong economic reforms. The analysis reveals the existence of a "Brady multiplier," where declines in overall debt burdens exceeded initial face value reductions. While similar mechanisms could again deliver substantial debt stock reductions during acute solvency crises, Brady-style solutions alone would not address current challenges related to creditor coordination, domestic reform barriers, and the rise of domestic debt, among others.

Keywords: Brady bonds, Brady Plan, debt relief, debt sustainability, sovereign debt restructuring

© Neil Shenai and Marijn A. Bolhuis 2026

ISBNs: 9781009747400 (HB), 9781009747431 (PB), 9781009747417 (OC)
ISSNs: 2753-9326 (online), 2753-9318 (print)

Contents

	Foreword	1
1	Introduction	2
2	Review of the Literature and an Overview of Debt and Debt Restructuring	8
3	The 1980s: A Decade of Sovereign Stress	23
4	Analyzing the Macroeconomic Impact of the Brady Plan	37
5	Policy Implications	69
6	Conclusions	86
	Appendix – Brady Options: Then and Now	90
	Abbreviations	92
	References	93

Foreword

In 1989, US Treasury Secretary Nicholas Brady announced a plan to restructure the debts of many heavily indebted emerging markets (EMs). The Brady Plan, as it came to be known, was a landmark initiative that offered deep debt haircuts to indebted countries while encouraging prudent economic reforms. Today, debt vulnerabilities are again on the rise, leading some observers to call for rebooting the original Brady Plan. But was the original Brady Plan truly a success? And if so, how and why did it succeed, and by what measures? What lessons can be drawn from it for the present period?

Neil Shenai and Marijn A. Bolhuis answer these urgent questions. They find that the Brady Plan was indeed a success, judged by the macroeconomic performance of Brady countries compared to peers. Their analysis reveals that overall debt burdens of Brady restructurers fell by much more than the initial debt relief provided – indicating the existence of a "Brady multiplier." The architects of the Brady Plan included the US Treasury International Affairs Under Secretary David Mulford and a team of outstanding civil servants, and this Element complements the empirical approach with meticulous historical research including several background discussions with the Brady Plan's original architects. Then, Shenai and Bolhuis explain the similarities and differences between the 1980s debt landscape and today. While they leave it up to readers to judge for themselves, it follows from their analysis that simply rebooting the Brady Plan today would not be a panacea to solve today's debt challenges. Should Brady-style mechanisms be considered, however, the authors helpfully provide clear insights into what this would entail.

Looking ahead, as of this writing, the future of the global economy is highly uncertain. Trade relationships are being redefined in real time. Many countries – including advanced economies – are grappling with high debt and low rates of economic growth. Meanwhile, major technological shifts are occurring amid waning social cohesion both within and among countries. Debt restructuring can be messy and rife with strategic interactions even in the best of times, with competing incentives among the official and private sectors, creditors and debtors, the international financial institutions (IFIs) and their constituents, and new players and incumbents.

In this context, Shenai and Bolhuis' work is a timely contribution for anyone interested in the original Brady Plan and its potential applicability today in a complex and constantly evolving sovereign debt restructuring architecture. What distinguishes this work is its ability to bridge scholarly rigor with accessibility. Readers – whether economists, policymakers, students, or those with a general interest in financial history – will find a thoughtful narrative that connects the technical with the political, the historical with the contemporary.

As a senior US Treasury official for nearly forty years, I recognized that the best solutions to global challenges, including on debt, blended ambition and pragmatism, along with realism and a belief in a better future. In a similar vein, this Element stands out for its skillful recognition of the Brady Plan's innovative aspects with a sober understanding of its limitations, avoiding both excessive praise and undue criticism. At a time when sovereign debt challenges are once again at the forefront of global concern, the lessons of the Brady Plan warrant renewed attention. Thanks to the authors, we now have an excellent guide.

-Mark Sobel

1 Introduction

In March 1989, US Treasury Secretary Nicholas Brady launched a plan for distressed sovereigns to restructure unsustainable debts via the issuance of so-called Brady bonds. Under Brady exchanges, creditors accepted face value and net present value (NPV) haircuts in exchange for greater assurances about debtors' capacity to repay, while debtors used the debt relief provided to restore debt sustainability and growth. Several inducements helped achieve voluntary creditor participation in Brady exchanges, including collateralized interest and principal payments of Brady bonds, debtors' commitments to economic reform under International Monetary Fund (IMF) programs, and the enhanced liquidity of the restructured claims. Overall, the original Brady Plan was viewed as a success as it reduced EM debt burdens, restored market access, diversified the EM creditor base, took illiquid loans off advanced economy (AE) commercial bank balance sheets and converted them into tradeable securities, and safeguarded economic reform momentum (EMTA, 2022).

This Element analyzes the macroeconomic impact of the Brady Plan. It finds that following the first Brady restructuring in 1990, Brady countries experienced substantial declines in their public and external debt burdens and a sharp pickup in output and productivity growth, anchored by their comparatively strong economic reform effort. In fact, the impact of Brady restructurings on overall debt burdens was many times greater than the initial face value reductions of the sovereign debt stocks, indicating the existence of a "Brady multiplier." Despite these favorable outcomes, Brady restructurings tended to take longer to complete than non-Brady restructurings and followed several years of debt rescheduling and liquidity relief, including via the Baker Plan.

Today, sovereign debt vulnerabilities are again on the rise. Considering this study's findings, Brady-style mechanisms could again be helpful in delivering meaningful debt stock reduction when debt solvency challenges are acute. However, Brady Plan-style mechanisms alone would not solve existing challenges in the sovereign debt landscape, including those related to creditor coordination, domestic barriers to economic reforms, and the increased prevalence of domestic debt, among others. To address these and other challenges, continued further progress on improving the international architecture for sovereign debt restructuring will be needed.

In the wake of the global financial crisis and the COVID-19 pandemic, many countries are dealing with large and costly debt overhangs. From 2008 to 2023, average AE public debt levels rose from about 79 percent to about 95 percent of GDP. Many EM and low-income countries (LICs) have experienced similar debt buildups since 2009 (see Figure 1). There is evidence that higher debt loads and tighter financial conditions are contributing to debt vulnerabilities. For example, as of end-2023 some 60 percent of LICs are at high risk of or in debt distress (Figure 2).[1] Many LICs are also experiencing a rise in debt servicing costs relative to government revenues, with the median external debt service to revenues ratio – a commonly used measure of liquidity pressures – rising from about 5 percent in 2010 to nearly 15 percent in 2023 (Holland & Pazarbasioglu, 2024).

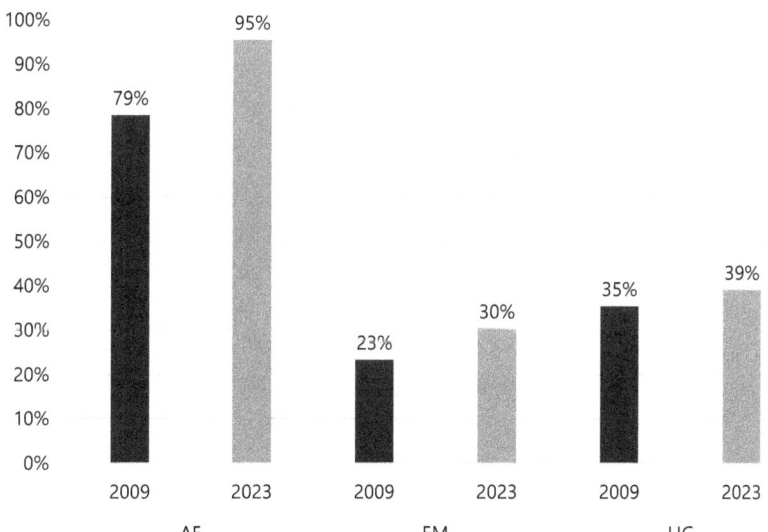

Figure 1 Debt-to-GDP ratios (by income group, percent of GDP)

Source: IMF World Economic Outlook Database and authors' calculations

---

[1] For an analysis of rising debt risks in the current period, see Chuku et al. (2023), World Bank (2022b), and Kose et al. (2022). On the evolution of external debt in low-income countries, see Setser (2025).

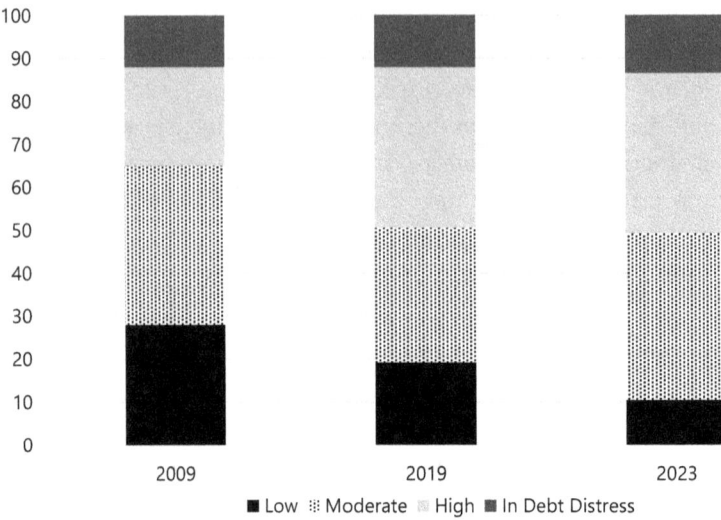

Figure 2 Risk of debt distress among LICs
Source: IMF LIC DSA database and authors' calculations (percent of total)

Higher debt vulnerabilities are taking place in the context of weaker global growth prospects, rising geoeconomic fragmentation, potentially "higher-for-longer" interest rates, reduced aid budgets, and a structural increase in spending pressures associated with climate change, supply chain resilience, and aging populations, among other factors (Rogoff, 2022) (Figures 3 and 4). Tighter global financial conditions today follow over a decade of low interest rates and a global reach for yield, in which many developing countries amassed considerable debt due to prolonged easy global financial conditions (Becker & Ivashina, 2014; Malpass, 2023). Global conditions are also becoming more shock-prone, as evidenced by the adverse spillovers from the COVID-19 pandemic and Russia's war in Ukraine (Georgieva, 2022). Should present trends persist, debt vulnerabilities could continue to grow. Sovereign debt challenges could in turn become more acute, with an increasing need to provide liquidity and solvency support via debt treatments to a broader swath of countries (International Monetary Fund, 2025a).[2]

Debt is neither inherently bad nor destabilizing. Used prudently, sovereign borrowing allows countries to pursue countercyclical economic policies, smooth consumption, and make critical investment in physical and human capital. Trouble emerges, however, when overall debt and debt service exceed

---

[2] See Arslanalp and Eichengreen (2023) on post-COVID debt levels. For a study of advanced economy debt vulnerabilities and the risk of fiscal dominance, see (Buiter, 2025).

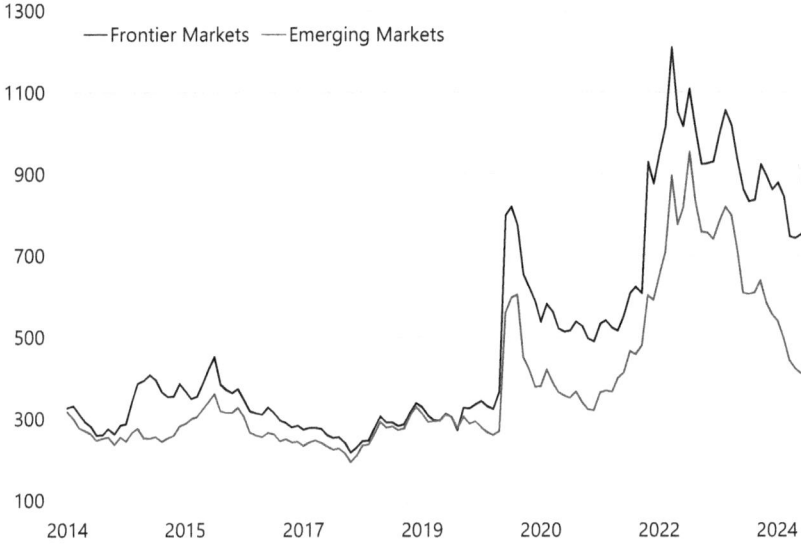

Figure 3 Sovereign spreads (basis points)

Source: Bloomberg terminal

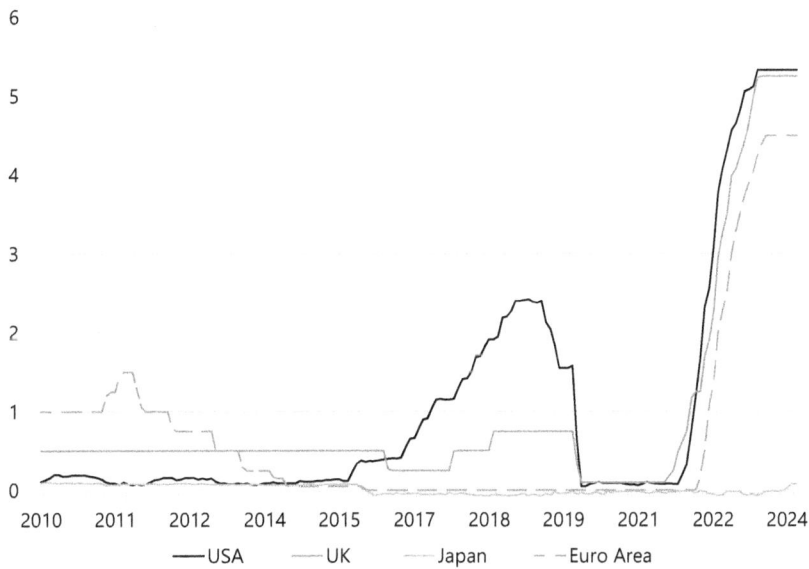

Figure 4 Advanced economy monetary policy rates (percent)

Source: Bloomberg terminal

the capacity of the sovereign to commit credibly to repay their borrowing. In some cases, countries may face liquidity pressures that make it difficult to service their debts, even if total sovereign assets available (i.e., the total potential revenue pool) exceed their liabilities. Other times, financing challenges become so severe that debt loads could become unsustainable given the feasible set of economic policies available to the country, creating a solvency challenge. In both cases, debtors may ask creditors to provide either liquidity or solvency relief to restore debt sustainability.

There is no bankruptcy mechanism available to sovereigns facing debt distress. Historically, sovereign debt restructuring thus occurred on a case-by-case and ad hoc basis. Debt restructurings can be complex, multistage, and multi-stakeholder negotiations, involving the debtor country, creditors both public and private, and multilateral institutions such as the IMF and other IFIs. During past periods of sovereign distress, official creditors coordinated their negotiations via forums such as the Paris Club, which delivered official sector debt treatments agreed on comparable terms. This mechanism facilitated private debt treatments and in turn catalyzed new financing for the sovereign with more sustainable debt burdens (Hagan, 2020).

The sovereign debt landscape has changed significantly since 2000. Creditor bases have become more heterogenous, with non-Paris Club and market-based financing, particularly for EMs, increasing significantly. As a result, achieving creditor coordination to deliver timely debt treatments has become more challenging.[3] Implementation of the Group of 20 (G20) Common Framework (CF) – a Paris Club-style forum in which G20 official creditors coordinate to provide debt relief on comparable terms – has faced challenges but has improved (Beaumont & Hakura, 2021; Pazarbasioglu, 2024). Meanwhile, the international financial architecture is beset with several preexisting challenges in sovereign debt resolution. Several authors argue that these limitations include the lack of a global sovereign debt restructuring mechanism (SDRM), uneven coverage of collective action clauses (CACs) of nonbonded debt – a gap that could allow minority holdout creditors to prevent debt treatments, the low uptake of contingent debt clauses, creditor and debtor debt transparency challenges, and a tendency for sovereign debt restructurings to undershoot at times the amount of debt relief required to restore sustainability, among other challenges.[4,5]

---

[3] See also Georgieva and Pazarbasioglu (2021), Neiman (2022), and Yellen (2023a), (2023b).

[4] SCDIs are option-like features embedded in sovereign debt contracts in which payments are linked to other variables, such as a country's GDP, the occurrence of natural disasters, or commodity prices. In some cases, they can provide useful insurance to issuers who may face repayment risks due to factors outside of their control, such as their country's susceptibility to natural disasters or global commodity price swings. As noted by the IMF, SCDIs can indeed pose challenges that can hamper their uptake, including challenges in pricing these instruments (and thus negatively impacting borrowing costs by leading borrowers to pay a liquidity premium) and moral hazard (International Monetary Fund, 2017). See also on IMF staff views regarding SCDIs in debt restructuring contexts (International Monetary Fund, 2020b) and (International Monetary Fund, 2024b).

[5] See, for instance, Hagan (2020), Malpass (2022), Sobel (2022), Bi, Chamon, & Zettelmeyer (2016), and Buchheit and Gulati (2020).

In this context, many analysts have argued that a more systemic approach to debt restructuring is needed, similar to the Brady Plan of 1989. The purpose of this Element is to examine the original Brady Plan in greater detail and draw lessons for the present period. It is relevant both to academics and policymakers interested in fiscal sustainability, sovereign debt, and debt restructuring, especially in the post-COVID context. It adds to the discussion of sovereign debt restructuring and the Brady Plan in three ways.

First, this Element analyzes how the original Brady Plan delivered on debt relief and growth for countries that undertook Brady-style debt treatments.[6] It does so by estimating the impact of the Brady Plan by comparing macroeconomic outcomes of ten Brady countries for which data are available to forty other emerging markets and developing economies (EMDEs) using difference-in-differences (DiD) and synthetic control approaches. This Element quantifies the macroeconomic impact of the Brady Plan, illustrating that the Brady Plan indeed delivered superior economic outcomes for Brady restructurers. Its empirical results show that Brady countries indeed achieved better outcomes than non-Brady peers. Brady restructurers tended to achieve lower public debt, lower external debt, higher growth, and lower inflation relative to the non-Brady control group. This is the first analysis to the authors' knowledge that employs econometric techniques such as difference-in-difference estimation and synthetic control methods (SCMs) to illustrate the macroeconomic impact of the Brady Plan.

Second, its results add to contemporary debates about the desirability of debt relief for heavily indebted countries. The findings indicate that Brady restructurers' reform effort likely contributed to their stronger macroeconomic outcomes relative to non-Brady peers. Indeed, this Element shows how the long-term impact of Brady face value reductions on debt levels was multiplied many times over – mainly driven by the more than doubling of the growth rate of Brady countries in the 1990s relative to the 1980s. This pickup in growth followed largely from total factor productivity (TFP) growth, which is consistent with a stronger structural reform effort in Brady countries.[7] This Element's results, therefore, indicate that debt relief coupled with strong reform efforts helped maximize the macroeconomic benefits of Brady-style restructurings. In other words, debt relief without

---

[6] Hereafter, the terms "Brady Plan" and "Brady restructurings" will be used interchangeably and refer to the suite of economic policy actions taken by debtors, creditors, and IFIs to reduce the face value of existing debt while undertaking complementary and related economic reforms.

[7] These primary results are confirmed via additional empirical checks.

a comparable reform effort may not lead to desirable macroeconomic outcomes.

Third, this Element presents policy implications of its analysis for sovereign debt restructuring today. In so doing, it shows that while Brady mechanisms may be useful in delivering meaningful face value haircuts for debtors, they alone are not sufficient to overcome existing challenges in today's sovereign debt restructuring landscape. Several features of today's sovereign debt landscape are also discussed.

The rest of this Element proceeds as follows. Section 2 provides a brief literature review, explaining the mechanics of debt sustainability and debt restructuring while summarizing prior studies of debt relief. Section 3 provides the historical context of the Brady Plan, discussing the rise of overseas lending by commercial banks in the 1970s followed by tightening financial conditions in the early 1980s, which led to sovereign debt challenges for many EM borrowers. This section explains how the Brady Plan was a culmination of almost ten years of concerted efforts to help distressed EM sovereigns deal with their debt overhangs. Section 4 presents this Element's empirical analysis, including a comparative study of the Brady restructurers and non-Brady peers. Section 5 examines the policy implications that follow from its empirical contribution. Section 6 concludes the Element. The Appendix provides a summary of the original Brady Plan options and potential options offered by other authors today.

2 Review of the Literature and an Overview of Debt and Debt Restructuring

This section briefly reviews the literature on debt sustainability and debt restructuring. It provides a technically accessible account of the main macroeconomic identities and theory underpinning debt sustainability analyses, explains why debt sustainability is important for macroeconomic stability, describes how to measure and assess debt sustainability, and highlights some related operational issues. Specifically, this section begins by defining debt sustainability and explaining its criticality to a country's overall macroeconomic stability. It discusses the key drivers of a country's fiscal path and explains some of the determinants of those drivers. This section also discusses the factors that determine a country's debt-carrying capacity, such as the depth of its financial sector and debt profile (encompassing elements such as the currency composition of debt and its duration). Thereafter, the section explains what happens when countries experience debt servicing difficulties, distinguishing between situations of illiquidity and insolvency. It explains the critical role of debt restructuring in reestablishing sovereigns' debt sustainability under both conditions. The section concludes with a discussion of previous studies of the Brady Plan. This section thus situates this Element within the broader literature and provides nontechnical background on its subsequent empirical analyses.

2.1 Principles of Debt Sustainability

Debrun et al. define debt as sustainable when a sovereign government "has a high probability of being solvent – that is, *able to honor its current and future financial obligations* – without having to resort to unfeasible or undesirable polices" (Debrun et al., 2020, p. 151).[8] The IMF classifies debt as unsustainable when "there are no politically and economically feasible policies that stabilize [a country's] debt-to-GDP ratio and deliver acceptably low rollover risk without restructuring and/or exceptional bilateral support" (International Monetary Fund, 2022a). Scholars such as Brunnermeier et al. argue that debt is considered solvent on an inter-temporal basis when the discounted NPV of future primary surpluses is equal to or greater the amount of contracted debt (Brunnermeier, Merkel, & Sannikov, 2020).[9] Should debt not be credibly backed by future primary surpluses, the sovereign can be considered insolvent, with potentially Ponzi-like debt dynamics (such that debts coming due are simply replaced with new borrowing, with little intention of the fiscal authority to repay the stock of debt).[10] Said another way, debt is considered unsustainable when a government's current policies, its macroeconomic trajectory, and its available set of feasible economic and political adjustment measures cannot yield a serviceable debt-to-GDP ratio over time.

While the above definitions are intuitive, scholars and practitioners have long struggled to operationalize assessments of debt sustainability. After all, sovereigns have the power to tax, which should give them ample fiscal space to

---

[8] Similarly, Dalia Hakura says debt as sustainable when "the government is able to meet all its current and future payment obligations without exceptional financial assistance or going into default" (Hakura, 2020).

[9] For a summary about debt risks in advanced economies and potential methods by which debt loads could be reduced, see Schuknecht (2022).

[10] For recent analyses on the degree to which fiscal expansions are "backed" by future primary surpluses, including how such distinctions relate to inflation, see (Anderson & Leeper, 2023) and (Cochrane, 2022).

service even high levels of debt. Furthermore, countries with debt denominated in their own currency and with autonomous monetary policy can in theory print money to repay maturing government obligations regardless of the size of maturing claims.[11] Thus, default should be impossible in such a circumstance. Still, the empirical record shows that sovereigns indeed periodically default, illustrating that their theoretically unlimited ability to tax and monetize debt faces practical limitations.

For example, Atish Ghosh et al. argued that there are several effectively binding constraints on the ability of a sovereign to restore debt sustainability via fiscal adjustment due to so-called fiscal fatigue, wherein the primary balance – or the government's revenue and expenditures net of interest expenditures – cannot keep increasing with rising debt. They in turn use their framework to compute empirical estimates of a primary balance reaction function to interest rates to assess country-specific debt limits and their related fiscal space given their current fiscal trajectories. These analyses have been used subsequently in operational work by the IMF and others such as Euro Area countries (Ghosh, Kim, Mendoza, Ostry, & Qureshi, 2013).[12] In cases where the sovereign is incapable of adjusting further due to fiscal fatigue and debt dynamics remain explosive, debt stock reduction would be needed to restore sustainability (i.e., a situation of insolvency).[13]

A common starting point for assessing debt sustainability is the *law of motion of debt* (equation (1)). This equation holds that the change in a country's debt stock for a given year (Δd_t) is a function of the real interest rate-growth differential ($r_t - g_t$), the rate of growth in nominal GDP ($1 + \pi_t + g_t$), the stock of debt from the preceding period (d_{t-1}), the government's primary fiscal balance (i.e., revenues less expenditures net of debt service, pb_t), and a residual term (o_t), all expressed as a percentage of GDP. The residual term (o_t) can encompass additional factors that impact a country's debt ratio, such as stock-flow adjustments, including differences between actual and recorded deficits, valuation effects (due to, for example, exchange rate impacts on foreign currency-denominated debt), recording effects, and other one-off changes to a government's debt ratio, which are often recorded "below-the-line" or outside of the perimeter of government revenues and expenditures.

---

[11] See, for example (Kelton, 2020) for the strong version of this argument known as "Modern Monetary Theory."
[12] On operational applications of this theory to fiscal space, see (Ostry et al., 2010).
[13] In the case of the Brady countries, the limits of adjustment were made clear over several years of MYRAs and the Baker period, where adjustment programs were premised on the idea that debt stock reduction was not needed and fiscal fatigue limits were nonbinding.

Examples of such below-the-line items include windfall gains from privatizations and other changes in government deposits or realizations of contingent liabilities (including from state-owned enterprises).[14]

Based on equation (1), debt will increase when the real interest rate-growth differential increases, the stock of inherited debt increases, when the growth rate in nominal GDP decreases, when the primary balance declines (or moves further into deficit), and when the residual term is positive.

$$\Delta d_t = \frac{r_t - g_t}{1 + \pi_t + g_t} d_{t-1} - pb_t + o_t. \qquad (1)$$

From the law of motion of debt accumulation, it is possible to derive a *debt-stabilizing primary balance* (pb_t^{DS}, see equation (2)), for which the expected change in debt is equal to 0. Note for the purposes of this analysis, the residual term is assumed to be 0.

$$pb_t^{DS} = \frac{r_t^* - \bar{g}_t}{1 + \bar{\pi} + \bar{g}_t} d_{t-1}. \qquad (2)$$

From this measure, it follows that if the current primary balance is less than its debt-stabilizing level, then debt will increase. If the primary balance is above the debt-stabilizing level, then debt will decrease. The debt-stabilizing primary balance is thus a useful benchmark for calibrating fiscal adjustment to restore debt sustainability: When setting medium-term fiscal policy, countries can choose a fiscal adjustment path to reach a certain debt target over time, conditional on a given interest-growth differential, steady-state inflation rate, and trend growth rate. Calibrating the level and pace of fiscal adjustment depends on several factors, such as the economic and political feasibility of raising tax revenues and cutting expenditures, as well as the expected implications of fiscal adjustment on growth (both actual and potential). For example, countries may be tempted to reduce capital expenditures to achieve a more sustainable fiscal balance. However, these actions may reduce the pace of investment, thereby reducing capital accumulation and in turn potential growth. Similarly, tax increases could adversely impact consumer demand, especially when levies hit consumers with relatively higher marginal propensities to consume. In turn, actual growth could fall due to the decline in consumption expenditures caused by higher taxes, ultimately reducing the amount of potential revenue raised. Therefore, appropriately calibrating fiscal consolidation requires a holistic judgment about the role of fiscal policy in the economy, with an eye toward

---

[14] On stock-flow adjustments and implications for government debt, see (Weber, 2012).

choosing tax and expenditure strategies that minimize inefficiencies and adverse spillovers.[15]

A key factor in determining how much debt a country can issue and service is its debt-carrying capacity. Several factors determine the total amount of debt that a country can issue, including investors' willingness to hold the sovereign's debt and, relatedly, the credibility of the existing fiscal path with current holders of sovereign debt. The ability of the domestic financial system to absorb government debt also determines debt-carrying capacity. Countries with more liquid and better capitalized financial systems have higher debt-carrying capacity, holding all else equal, as their financial institutions have more space to better absorb debt issued by the sovereign (Hakura, 2020). Other financial market factors, such as capital requirements, can also impact a country's debt-carrying capacity. Government debt is often treated as a safe asset for regulatory capital purposes, such that higher capital requirements increase demand for safe assets, including government debt (Crosignani, 2021).

In addition to targeting a specific debt-to-GDP level, some authors such as Jason Furman and Larry Summers argue that in certain circumstances, including when real interest rates are anticipated to be lower-for-longer, a better metric of assessing fiscal sustainability could be the sovereign's total interest expense as a percentage of GDP. Said another way, the total ratio of debt-to-GDP may be high, but if declining real interest rates offset the higher debt stock, such that debt service as a percentage of GDP is unchanged, then fiscal sustainability would not necessarily be adversely impacted (Furman & Summers, 2020). These considerations are particularly relevant in a low-for-long interest rate environment but may be less applicable in a world where real interest rates are greater than real growth rates.[16]

A sovereign's debt profile also has implications for the extent of fiscal risks posed by debt. Debt held by relatively more fickle investor bases – such as from potentially flighty foreign investors – is often seen as more likely to succumb to run dynamics. Similarly, debt denominated in foreign currency poses both run risk and currency risk, such that currency depreciation raises the real value of foreign currency debt burdens. This risk is compounded by the fact that often sovereign governments cannot borrow from foreign investors in their local currency. As a result, they issue debt in foreign currency, subjecting them to currency mismatches and the risk of capital flight

---

[15] For a study of the impact on fiscal consolidation on the output of 16 Organization of Economic Co-operation and Development (OECD) countries, including potential monetary policy responses, see (Alesina et al., 2016). On the composition of consolidation, see also (Carnot, 2013).

[16] See also (Blanchard, 2023).

(Eichengreen & Hausmann, 1999). Longer-term debt is considered safer because roll-over risk is lower, although this safety tends to carry a price in the form of term and other premia.

2.2 Elements of Debt Distress and Debt Restructuring

Having described the principles of debt sustainability, this section now discusses how sovereigns can preempt and react to sovereign stress. It explains under what conditions governments may undertake fiscal adjustment to improve debt sustainability and then distinguishes between periods of illiquidity and insolvency, with the latter tending to require larger effort from existing creditors to restore sustainability. Emphasis is placed on the role of official creditors in facilitating debt restructuring processes as well as common operational challenges in achieving debt restructurings. The section also briefly covers several emerging topics in debt distress and restructuring, such as the role of credit enhancements and value recovery instruments (VRIs) in debt restructuring.

When a country faces debt challenges – for instance, due to rising debt service burdens that crowd out other priority spending or when investors lose faith in the country's existing fiscal path and potentially limit the ability of the government to refinance its debt obligations – it can try to undertake fiscal consolidation to restore fiscal space and achieve a more sustainable debt trajectory. There are several modalities and additional considerations related to fiscal consolidation to achieve debt reduction, including the pace and duration of adjustment, the impact of consolidation on growth (i.e., fiscal multipliers), credibility with the market, and adjustment fatigue (with larger fiscal efforts being harder to maintain, all other things equal). If these actions are deemed credible by the market and can be sustained, then adjustment can be sufficient to restore debt sustainability (Best et al., 2019).[17]

However, adjustment alone is sometimes insufficient to reduce sovereign stress. Rather, governments may face liquidity challenges that make it difficult to service existing obligations at reasonable rates. A country with large gross financing needs (either domestic or external) could face liquidity pressures if, for example, market participants doubted the sovereign's ability to commit credibly to a sustainable fiscal path while, at the same time, the government had inadequate buffers to carry it through a financing shock. Lumpiness in the debt repayment profile, such as bunched amortization (i.e., principal) payments coming due can indicate future liquidity strains, especially if global financial

---

[17] Best et al. (2019) also discuss monetary and financial policy responses to reduce debt, such as when the monetary authority uses monetary policy to help reduce debt or when the fiscal authority engages in financial repression to tax savings to achieve a debt reduction.

conditions lead to prohibitively expensive financing costs. Additional indicators of potential liquidity risks include the structure of the existing sovereign debt stock, with shorter-term, externally financed debt (particularly in hard currency) posing the greatest potential for exacerbating liquidity strains. Another measure of liquidity is the amount of short-term debt coming due relative to cash and cash-like assets on hand to make these payments. For external debt, international reserves relative to short-term debt on a remaining maturity basis is a useful liquidity measure as well.

Other times, a government may face solvency pressures, which is related to overall debt sustainability. When a country experiences a solvency problem, its ability to make future payments is outweighed by future feasible revenue collection. Solvency analysis also requires an assessment of the government's implicit liabilities in addition to its explicit (contractual and debt related) ones. Such implicit liabilities could come from the private sector, including banks, local governments, and unfunded pension and other social spending-related obligations (Sturzenegger & Zettelmeyer, 2006, pp. 297–302). In any event, when a government is insolvent, it does not have the means to service its debt even under an ambitious adjustment scenario.

When either liquidity or solvency challenges emerge, including when a country is on the brink of losing market access, a government may seek a debt treatment from its existing creditors to reduce sovereign stress and, if needed, restore medium-term sustainability. Several options are available to a sovereign in potential distress, including achieving debt flow relief to address near-term liquidity strains, such as by capitalizing interest payments coming due. They can also seek principal write-downs via face value reductions to decrease the total stock of sovereign debt outstanding. Assuming constant discount rates for pre- and post-restructuring scenarios, face value reductions tend to lead to bigger NPV haircuts for the borrower (and thus require a greater effort on behalf of creditors to deliver these savings to debtors). As explained by IMF (2013), debt restructurings often provide too little debt relief too late, which can hamper the ability of the sovereign to restore sustainability via restructuring. This tendency reflects incentives to play for time for both creditors and debtors: Creditors are often willing to give a distressed sovereign time to adjust or pass losses onto other creditor classes so that they can avoid taking losses, while debtors are often loath to bear the costs of restructuring unless they are unavoidable (International Monetary Fund, 2013). Indeed, as explained in the next section, these incentives to play for time were present among many of Latin America's distressed sovereigns and their creditors in the 1980s, which was generally seen as a period of "extend and pretend" prior to the launch of the Brady Plan. In any event, the goal of a debt restructuring is to provide sufficient debt relief to restore sustainability, ensure adequate burden sharing among existing creditors, country authorities, and IFIs, such as the IMF, and be achieved in a timely manner.[18]

The decision to request a debt restructuring is the purview of the debtor. Once a country decides to restructure its debts, there are several steps in achieving an agreement with its creditors, with the IMF often playing a decisive role in the process. Sovereigns usually engage and retain their own legal and financial advisors to help them with their debt restructuring. These advisors help the country take an inventory of the stock of debt and reconciling this data with individual creditors, as well as develop a restructuring and communications strategy. Critically, it is necessary to determine the total amount of debt relief needed to restore sustainability for the country. This judgment is usually informed by IMF staff's debt sustainability analysis which, together with a developed macroeconomic adjustment program for the distressed sovereign, helps determine the total amount of debt relief required to restore sustainability. While the IMF staff will identify the total amount of debt relief required to restore sustainability, its staff will not comment on modalities of burden sharing among creditors.[19] Thus, debtor countries – under close advisement from their legal and financial advisors – will decide on a course of action to engage different classes of creditors, including mechanisms to negotiate with official bilateral creditors such as through the CF or Paris Club.

It is key at this stage to achieve the right balance of financing (both new financing such as from IMF programs and debt relief) as well as debtor actions via adjustment: Too little adjustment and too much financing could presage future debt distress challenges, while too much adjustment and too little financing could prove economically and politically unsustainable and, ultimately, self-defeating by impairing the capacity of the distressed sovereign to repay. Achieving the right combination between adjustment and new financing, including the debt relief envelope, is both an art and a science, but also a needed major factor in the design of IMF-supported adjustment programs.

Advisors will also help the debtor decide on the pool of debt that can be included in a restructuring (i.e., the "perimeter" of the restructuring). Senior debt to IFIs is not included in the restructuring perimeter due to their so-called preferred creditor status (PCS).[20] Additionally, countries may prefer to forego

---

[18] As argued by Lazard, one of the principles of prudent sovereign debt restructuring is to balance competing incentives regarding the timeliness of restructuring: debt relief offered too quickly may fuel moral hazard concerns, while delayed relief could lead to prolonged macroeconomic distress and scarring. Identifying consensus timelines for debt relief is complicated, with different preferences across stakeholders (see (Lazard, 2025a)).

[19] For more on the role of the IMF in debt restructuring, see IMF (2024b), especially pages 49–62.

[20] The seniority of a claim refers to its relative order in which it will be repaid by the sovereign. In a default event, more senior creditors are paid first. Typically, IFI claims are the highest in seniority

including domestic debt in the restructuring perimeter, as doing so could impose losses on vulnerable groups such as households or otherwise impair credit markets and bank health, thereby proving more costly to growth and financial stability than the potential benefits of debt relief (Grigorian, 2023). On the other hand, pushing domestic debt restructuring may be preferred to mitigate reputational costs of requesting external debt restructuring and may be easier to achieve due to the sovereign's ability to change domestic law (and thus the terms of their domestic obligations) without protracted negotiations.[21] Advice from advisors and IMF staff can help debtors consider these trade-offs in the formulation of their restructuring strategy.

Advisors will also help the distressed debtor determine an appropriate cutoff date after which new financing is not included in the restructuring perimeter. Cutoff dates have the benefit of preserving assurances to creditors that near-term financing will not be "bailed in" even for a country in debt distress, thereby preserving critical financing during the restructuring period (Global Sovereign Debt Roundtable, 2025).

The IMF's lending framework requires that programs are fully financed and hence the IMF staff's debt sustainability analysis plays a central role in determining the financing envelope needed by the sovereign to restore debt sustainability. This condition reflects the requirement that IMF lending should restore medium-term external viability for its members while doing so under adequate safeguards, as per the IMF's *Articles of Agreement*. External financing gaps in the baseline macroeconomic framework would not restore external viability even with adjustment envisaged under the IMF program and creditor actions. Thus, the IMF will seek "financing assurances" from official sector creditors that any debt treatments required under the program will be offered in a manner consistent with the IMF's macroeconomic framework and debt sustainability analysis for a distressed sovereign. These financing assurances are required for IMF programs to be approved by the IMF Executive Board (Makoff, Maret, & Wright, 2025). Operationalizing these assurances, including from new creditors, has been a major multilateral focus in recent years, such as through refinements to the IMF's debt policies.[22]

IMF staff collaborates with debtors and creditors – both official and private – to provide a baseline macroeconomic assessment of the debtor country and to identify the requirements for restoring debt sustainability. These debt targets flow through to several aspects of restructuring negotiations, including the need

---

based on the norm of PCS. For more information on the PCS of the international financial institutions, including the IMF, see Martha (1990) and, more recently, Lazard (2025b).

[21] For IMF staff views on restructuring domestic debt, see International Monetary Fund (2021b).

[22] See International Monetary Fund (2024b).

for financing assurances. Targets include reaching certain debt-to-GDP ratios by the end of the IMF program period or bringing flow indicators such as debt-to-exports or debt service-to-revenues below a critical threshold in the relevant IMF debt sustainability framework for the country in question. Achieving these targets would be facilitated by the economic reform program envisaged by the IMF program, including the qualitative and quantitative conditionality embedded in the program (International Monetary Fund, 2024b).

Agreeing on an ultimate treatment with creditors can often be a protracted process depending on creditor classes. In general, official sector engagement takes place through international forums such as the Paris Club and, recently, the G20's CF, which followed the Debt Service Suspension Initiative (DSSI). Paris Club principles such as solidarity, consensus, information sharing, pursuing a case-by-case approach, conditionality and adjustment, and achieving comparability of treatment help promote cooperative outcomes, reduce free riding, and encourage sustainable policies by debtors. Debtors may also choose to engage official creditors individually, though doing so may complicate negotiations and extend restructuring timelines.

Commercial creditors are often dealt with on a case-by-case basis or via representative creditor committees. Bondholders will usually form bondholder committees, which will negotiate with the sovereign and negotiate terms of the restructuring. Debtors can offer a consent solicitation to bondholders, which requires a critical threshold of creditors to approve the new terms of the restructured bonds. The deployment of CACs has improved processes for restructuring by reducing holdout and litigation risks and making it easier for private creditors to come to terms with the distressed debtor.

During negotiations, carrots and sticks can be used to forge consensus on a restructuring. Carrots include cash sweeteners, VRIs, such as claims on future commodity revenue streams, loss reinstatement features (which allow creditors to claw back some debt relief offered if a subsequent restructuring is requested), parity of treatment undertakings, credit enhancements (such as those employed during the Brady Plan), and contractual improvements. Sticks may also be employed during negotiations, including threats of nonpayment, employing CACs to deal with holdout creditors, changing local laws to achieve more favorable terms, exit consents (which allow a qualified majority of creditors to modify aspects of original claims to make them less attractive to holdout creditors), using trust structures, and protecting assets from creditor seizure (Buchheit et al., 2019).

Some commentators have argued that state-contingent debt instruments could be useful tools to speed restructuring when creditors disagree about the borrower's prospects for recovery. While operationalizing restructured debt with state-contingent features can be challenging – due to data quality issues or liquidity premia – they can potentially be used to reduce uncertainty and speed restructurings (Neiman, 2023). VRIs were used in recent restructuring cases, including in Suriname, Sri Lanka, and Zambia, though there are design issues with VRIs that need to be considered (Panizza, 2024).[23]

While theoretically straightforward, there are myriad operational challenges in debt restructuring, which reflect the complex interplay of different players and several layers of strategic interaction, including vis-à-vis the sovereign and its creditors and intra-creditor dynamics.

First is the ability of the distressed sovereign to commit credibly to a macroeconomic stabilization plan amid a debt crisis to unlock new financing via debt relief and financial flows from IFIs. Often, the domestic political barriers or practical infeasibility to policy adjustment can undermine the effectiveness of a macroeconomic stabilization plan, even if the sovereign authorities are willing to pursue it. For instance, as discussed previously, governments can experience fiscal fatigue, where the primary balance can no longer respond to rising levels of public debt. These pressures can be particularly acute when the distressed sovereign must undertake growth-enhancing reforms, often in an environment of limited fiscal space.

Second, creditor coordination challenges could make timely and predictable restructurings difficult to achieve. The rise of non-Paris Club creditors, coupled with the ability of some LICs to tap international markets via Eurobond issuances and sovereign loans, has made the international creditor landscape more diverse and thus creditor coordination at times more challenging.[24] Additionally, the presence of plurilateral institutions could complicate the recognition of PCS, with more institutions claiming PCS potentially leading to the "multiplication of 'sanctuarised creditors,'" as argued by Lazard.[25] Continued further efforts to enhance creditor coordination are helping facilitate more timely and predictable restructurings, and these efforts should continue.

Third, as mentioned previously, there are often systematic incentives for both creditors and debtors to play for time, which can lead to "extend and pretend" debt workouts and serial restructurings. Changing these fundamental incentives facing creditors and their debtors will take time.

Fourth, the role of domestic debt can complicate debt restructurings. On the one hand, the availability of deep and liquid domestic savings bases can be

---

[23] For more on state-contingent features in restructurings, see International Monetary Fund (2024b), especially Appendix X.
[24] On the changing creditor landscape and creditor coordination challenges, including international responses, see Chabert, Cerisola, & Hakura (2022).
[25] See Lazard (2025a) and Lazard (2025b).

useful for the sovereign to smooth consumption and build out a yield curve to catalyze additional credit extension to the private sector. On the other hand, domestic exposure to the sovereign could create challenges in the debt restructuring context, as domestic savers may not be able to take losses imposed by a restructuring at a reasonable cost to their financial health and to overall macroeconomic dynamics – a limitation understood by the private sector. For example, Lazard, a sovereign debt advisor for many countries facing debt distress, argues that from the perspective of the private sector, domestic debt restructuring is not necessarily beneficial for external creditors, as it remains unclear whether there is a positive relationship between domestic debt relief and a country's ability to generate foreign exchange revenue to repay external creditors (Lazard, 2025a).[26] In any event, the rise and prevalence of domestic debt markets is a key distinction between the Brady period and today.

Fifth, care must be taken to protect new financing available to the sovereign during the restructuring context, often by setting cutoff dates for codifying the restructuring perimeter at an appropriate time to incentivize new financing. This practice provides adequate assurances to new creditors that their financing will not face haircuts. Such a mechanism is useful in preserving the sovereign's access to critical short-term financing, such as trade finance.

Sixth, achieving adequate burden sharing among different creditor classes can be difficult, particularly regarding comparability of treatment. In general, greater diversity of creditors can complicate comparability assessments, with different creditor classes preferring different measures of comparability of treatment.

Recent efforts by the Global Sovereign Debt Roundtable (GSDR) have helped clarify common understanding on many of these issues, including with new creditor classes particularly in the official sector. For instance, the GSDR has helped establish guidance on information sharing related to debt sustainability analyses in restructuring. It has also helped clarify that short-term debt (i.e., debt with an original maturity of one year or less) is generally excluded from restructuring perimeters and that so-called cutoff dates are appropriately calibrated to preserve new financing available for a distressed sovereign. The GSDR has also helped achieve common understanding related to the costs and benefits of domestic debt restructuring and nonresident holders of domestic debt. Operationally, the GSDR helped clarify comparability of treatment assessments in both CF and non-CF restructuring cases, including sensitivity analyses using multiple discount rates. It has also clarified mutual understanding related

---

[26] On the other hand, including domestic debt in the restructuring perimeter offers the benefit to the external private sector of having a potentially larger pool of restructurable debt, with the creditor effort required to provide debt relief spread out among more classes of creditors.

to debt swaps and climate resilient debt instruments, engagement with credit rating agencies (CRAs), SCDIs, and debt service suspension and the treatment of arrears, among other topics (Global Sovereign Debt Roundtable, 2024). The progress made by the GSDR illustrates the critical importance of multilateral coordination and constructive policy innovation in facilitating sovereign debt restructurings.

2.3 Other Analyses of the Brady Plan

Several authors have studied the impact of the Brady Plan previously. For instance, Gumbau-Brisa and Mann (2009) argue that Brady restructurings improved the market for distressed sovereign debt by improving solvency and better aligning prices with fundamentals, rather than short-run factors such as sentiment. Moreover, Brady restructurers also undertook economic reforms before and after restructurings that were seen as growth- and credit-enhancing (EMTA, 2022), including those reforms envisaged, urged, and helped implemented by the World Bank. As argued by Arslanalp and Henry (2005), Brady treatments led to significant stock market appreciations in Brady restructuring countries relative to the control group. The authors also show that Brady restructurings were not a zero-sum game between creditors and debtors: Commercial banks with significant developing country loan exposure (i.e., those most exposed to Brady restructurers) experienced a notable rise in their market capitalization relative to a control group of financial institutions.[27] Reinhart and Trebesch (2016) estimate that Brady countries experienced a substantial reduction in public debt levels and significantly faster economic growth after the first Brady restructuring in 1990. More recently, Jérôme Sgard published an interdisciplinary account of the 1980s sovereign debt crisis, with an analysis of the Baker and Brady Plans. Drawing on historical archives and interviews, Sgard's account describes how the IMF evolved to adopt a more active role in sovereign debt restructurings. He too identifies the Brady Plan as a success, insofar as it restored sustainability for Brady restructurers (Sgard, 2023).[28]

---

[27] As found by Arslanalp and Henry (2005), when developing countries announced debt relief agreements under the Brady Plan, their stock markets appreciated by an average of 60 percent in real dollar terms – a $42 billion increase in shareholder value. There is no significant stock market increase for a control group of countries that do not sign Brady agreements. The stock market appreciations successfully forecast higher future resource transfers, investment, and growth. Since the market capitalization of US commercial banks with developing country loan exposure also rose in this case – by $13 billion – the study's results suggest that both borrowers and lenders can benefit from debt relief when the borrower suffers from an unsustainable debt overhang.

[28] This Element complements Sgard's analysis by providing a more empirically based perspective on the original Brady Plan.

Others disagree about the efficacy of the Brady Plan. Vásquez (1996) highlighted that non-Brady reformers, such as Colombia and Chile, tended to have strong performance despite not receiving a Brady treatment. Similarly, Berthélemy and Lensink (1992) found heterogeneity in the economic performance of Brady restructurers and argued that the short-term growth effects of Brady restructurings were limited.

One of the distinct benefits of this Element relative to prior studies is its use of novel empirical techniques to demonstrate the efficacy of the Brady Plan, including DiD and SCM approaches. Additionally, few prior studies have attempted to link structural reform efforts of Brady restructurers with their macroeconomic outcomes, which is a major focus of this Element (which looks at IMF program performance of Brady countries using a dataset on IMF programs theretofore not used systematically to assess Brady restructurers). It also uses additional novel metrics of reform efforts. No empirical study of the Brady Plan to date has analyzed its applicability to the current sovereign debt architecture, which is also a focus of this Element.

Recent events have also rekindled interest in Brady-style mechanisms to address debt vulnerabilities. Lee Buchheit and Adam Lerrick recently proposed a Brady bond-style exchange structure in which low-income and other debt-vulnerable governments restructure the entire stock of their external debt under one of two Brady-like structures, including a cash down-payment structure or a floor of support structure (see Appendix).[29] The authors argue that the Brady Plan experience indicated that debt crises can be arrested with a "template transaction structure" to catalyze official support and stretch out interest and principal repayments (Buchheit & Lerrick, 2023). Brahima S. Coulibaly and Wafa Abedin similarly argued that the World Bank and IMF could manage a Brady-style debt exchange mechanism for heavily indebted countries eligible for the G20 CF to reduce debt loads via the issuance of Recovery and Sustainability bonds (Coulibaly & Abedin, 2023). Ying Qian also claimed that Brady-like restructurings could be useful in reducing post-COVID sovereign debt loads while enhancing the resilience of debt portfolios by introducing, for example, SCDIs or commodity-linked provisions to the restructured bonds (Qian, 2021).[30] During the European sovereign debt crisis in the 2010s, Nicholas Economides and Roy C. Smith argued that so-called Trichet Bonds (named after then-ECB President Jean-Claude Trichet) could be used to resolve

---

[29] The cash down-payment structure would guarantee an up-front payment to the creditor for agreeing to restructure, while the floor of support structure would include a highly rated zero-coupon financial instrument that collateralizes the restructured bond. See also Wolf (2022) for a summary of the Buchheit–Lerrick plan.

[30] SCDIs and other commodity-linked structures were used in some Brady restructurings as well.

unsustainable debts, suggesting that the European Central Bank could manage debt exchanges of distressed Euro Area countries' loans using collateralized bonds.[31] Some quarters of civil society have called for systemic debt relief. For example, Barbados Prime Minister Mia Mottley argued that the world required a "Jubilee moment" or "debt cancellation policy" given climate risks and financing needs (Politico EU, 2024). More recently, the late Pope Francis called for strong multilateral action on debt, possibly including debt relief (Vatican News, 2025).

While these recent perspectives deserve credit for their bold thinking, they raise several unanswered questions. Authors such as Buchheit and Lerrick and Coulibaly and Abedin do not spell out how and why the original Brady Plan delivered on debt relief and enabled better macroeconomic outcomes for Brady restructurers, taking its benefit for debtors as given. In reality, the track record of debt relief in catalyzing lasting growth is mixed.[32] These authors also do not explain the underlying mechanisms by which Brady exchanges can lead to better outcomes relative to alternative approaches available today, such as the G20's CF. To the extent that Buchheit and Lerrick attempt to account for the causal links between Brady treatments and better outcomes, they tend to focus primarily on the debt relief aspects of the original Brady Plan, rather than other planks of Brady restructurings, such as debtor actions like undertaking economic reforms to qualify for Brady treatments. These accounts tend to minimize differences among target debtor countries, failing to explain why a mechanism originally designed for EMs with market access (i.e., Brady restructurers) would be well-suited to helping today's LICs. They also do not discuss the changing creditor landscape, including the rise of non-Paris Club creditors and market-based financing (e.g., Eurobonds and bank loans) and related challenges with creditor coordination. Debt profiles look different today as well, with domestic debt playing a larger role. Moreover, many countries experience considerable domestic barriers to economic reforms, especially when the benefits are perceived to be delayed, with large up-front political costs.

2.4 Summary

This section summarized the literature on sovereign debt and debt restructuring. It emphasized the critical role of sovereign borrowing in allowing countries to pursue countercyclical polices, smooth consumption, and make critical investments. The section described the principles of debt sustainability, grounding the

---

[31] Under this scheme, the European Central Bank would issue zero-coupon bonds to serve as collateral for restructured sovereign claims of Euro Area members, see (Economides & Smith, 2011).

[32] See, for example (Easterly, 2002), especially chapter 7.

analysis in the law of motion of debt. From this equation, it is possible to assess debt dynamics by decomposing the change in a country's debt-to-GDP ratio into the real interest rate paid on its debt, trend real growth rate, inflation rate, existing debt stock, primary balance, and other items (such as one-time charges, stock-flow adjustments, etc.). In addition to these medium-term debt dynamics, a country's debt-carrying capacity helps determine how much it can borrow: Countries with more debt-carrying capacity (due to, for instance, the depth of their financial markets) can issue more debt, holding all else equal. Another key factor in determining the likelihood of sovereign stress is the country's sovereign debt profile, with debt held by relatively more fickle investor bases or denominated in foreign currency more likely to pose problems for the sovereign.

After describing these principles of debt sustainability, the section outlined the elements of debt distress and restructuring. It distinguished between liquidity and solvency pressures, with the latter requiring more effort from existing creditors (i.e., relief offered) to restore debt sustainability. Sovereigns can try to forestall debt treatments by adjusting their primary balance path. When adjustment alone is insufficient to restore sustainability, countries can request debt treatments from their existing creditors. The steps in debt restructuring were then discussed, including determining the total amount and type of debt relief required to restore sustainability, as informed by a debt sustainability analysis often performed by IMF staff. Thereafter, the total perimeter of sovereign debt to be restructured (the "perimeter") must be decided, with restructuring often requiring a mix of new financing, macroeconomic adjustment, and changed terms on the existing debt stock (i.e., restructuring). Negotiations can employ a variety of carrots and sticks. The section also recognized operational challenges in debt restructuring and recent effort to address these challenges, including through the GSDR. The section closed with a summary of existing studies of the Brady Plan, in turn situating this Element in the broader literature.

3 The 1980s: A Decade of Sovereign Stress

This section provides historical context for the Brady Plan. It begins by describing the nature and evolution of global capital markets from the end of World War II, through the original Bretton Woods period of fixed exchange rates and capital flow restrictions, and into the end of Bretton Woods and beginning of a period of capital mobility. It describes the role that global banks played in allocating capital to many EM countries and how the Volcker shock of the early 1980s led to a major capital flow reversal, leading to lost market access and debt distress. As many Latin American and other EM countries fell into crises, the global response initially treated these pressures as a liquidity rather than solvency problem. After nearly a decade of efforts on behalf of IFIs and debtor countries to provide liquidity support and help rebuild lenders' balance sheets, in 1989 US Treasury Secretary Nicholas Brady pushed for the Brady Plan. By describing these historical antecedents to the Brady Plan, this section contextualizes the empirical analyses and policy implications that follow in Sections 4 and 5.

3.1 Historical Developments

The roots of the Latin American debt crisis and Brady Plan lay in macroeconomic and financial developments in the global economy in the decades following the end of World War II. Following the war, AEs adopted a fixed exchange rate standard with financial account restrictions amid a broader push for trade liberalization, anchored by the US dollar as the key currency, which itself was pegged to the value of gold at $35 per troy ounce. This system – known as the original Bretton Woods system, or "Bretton Woods I" – was relatively stable during the early postwar years, enabled by the strong performance of the US economy. The United States' dominant international position led to a global dollar shortage, as many European countries ran large current account deficits (with a concomitant need for foreign capital) to reconstruct their economies, build capacity, and grow through exports. Partially to address this dollar shortage (within its broader strategic imperatives), the United States undertook a robust reconstruction policy via the Marshall Plan, providing the necessary funds to facilitate Europe's reconstruction (Bordo, 1992).[33]

By the late 1950s and early 1960s, the United States began to run smaller balance of payments surpluses, driven by the European recovery and a related reduction in its trade balance and current account, which ultimately swung into deficit in the 1970s amid the Vietnam War and subsequent oil price shocks. The alleviation of the global dollar shortage and switch to a regime of a global dollar surplus had major implications for the Bretton Woods fixed exchange rate regime and for global finance. Toward the end of the 1950s, flush with dollars generated by the widening US current account deficit, many UK-based banks pushed to develop various Eurodollar and eurocurrency markets, in which non-US based financial centers and borrowers issued non-local currency debts, in turn enhancing the ability of countries and firms to borrow in global markets (Ocampo, 2017, pp. 112–113). These developments

---

[33] For more on the Marshall Plan, see (Steil, 2018).

reflected both Europe's recovery and the relative surplus of dollars held by banks abroad.

By the end of the 1960s, the surge in dollars held abroad dwarfed the pool of gold available for the United States to redeem at the fixed value of $35 per ounce. Additionally, by this time, Europe and Japan largely rebuilt their industrial bases, with their firms making steady inroads into the American market. As a result, American firms and their Congressional representatives had been advocating for more protectionist measures to shield American producers from foreign competition, enabled by the unsustainably strong dollar vis-à-vis America's trading partners. By August 1971, US President Richard Nixon announced a series of measures that ended the convertibility of the dollar for gold and, with it, effectively devalued the dollar (Calleo, 1981). In parallel, President Nixon also introduced a tariff surcharge of 10 percent on dutiable imports, a $6.3 billion tax cut financed by commensurately reduced expenditures, and a ninety-day price freeze (Irwin, 2012). With a de facto global reserve standard based on the US dollar and, in 1973, floating exchange rates, this era came to be known as "Bretton Woods II" (Wolf, 2008, pp. 81–82), (Irwin & Obstfeld, 2024). During this period, international capital mobility picked up as countries reduced capital account restrictions and opened their markets to foreign capital.

Bank lending to EMDEs, mainly in Latin America, rose dramatically during the following decade. The 1970s saw a series of oil and commodity price shocks associated with the Organization of Arab Petroleum Exporting Countries oil embargo on the United States in 1973 following the Yom Kippur War and, later, the oil shock associated with a decline in Iranian output due to the Iranian Revolution in 1979 (Corbett, 2013; Graefe, 2013). Due to these events, US dollar-denominated petroleum prices rose over ten-fold from 1970 to 1980. A representative commodity basket nearly quadrupled in price over the same period (see Figure 5).

This increase in export earnings among commodity producers led to large balance of payments surpluses in oil-exporting countries, which deposited their foreign exchange earnings in US commercial banks. In turn, banks lent to Latin American sovereigns, with the total stock of outstanding debt rising from about $30 billion in 1970 to $330 billion by 1982 (Sims & Romero, 2013). Many of these loans had variable rate (or "floating") interest rate structures: Thus, as interest rates rose, so too did interest payments (Skidmore, Smith, & Green, 2010, pp. 368–375). Still, from the viewpoint of external sustainability, many Latin American borrowers appeared to have sustainable policies. For instance, their current account balances remained at or near surplus in the early 1970s, while the stock of their

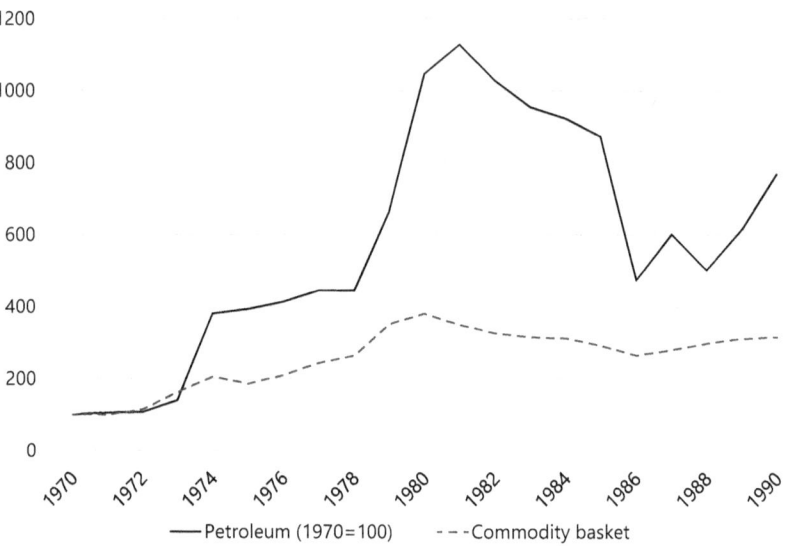

Figure 5 Petroleum and commodity prices (1970–90)
Source: Bloomberg terminal

net external liabilities as measured by their net international investment positions (NIIP) hovered around negative 20 percent of GDP.[34]

Ultimately, inadequate US macroeconomic policy and successive waves of price shocks in the 1970s led to a significant monetary tightening in the United States in the early 1980s, championed by Federal Reserve Chairman Paul Volcker (Blinder, 2022, pp. 117–132). This Volcker shock was the start of a steep tightening cycle in global financial conditions. From 1976 through 1981, the federal funds rate rose from about 5 percent to over 16 percent. Higher US interest rates contributed to a strengthening of the US dollar, with the US dollar index rising over 30 percent from 1980 through 1986 (see Figure 6).

As global financial conditions tightened and the world economy entered a recession in 1981, many Latin American countries lost market access and could no longer service their debts as commercial banks retrenched their lending. This capital flow reversal in the early 1980s coincided with a decline in commodity prices for many key exports in the region. An index of commodity prices declined by about 50 percent from 1979 through 1984 (see Figure 5). The associated funding squeeze led to debt sustainability and external sustainability challenges for many heavily indebted Latin American countries. The average

---

[34] For a recent analysis of international investment incomes as they relate to countries' balance of payments, see (Joyce, 2025).

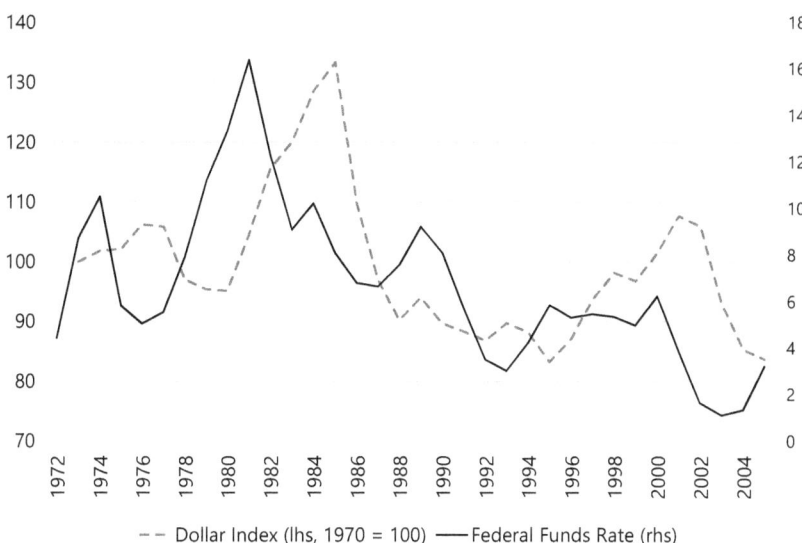

Figure 6 US dollar index and the federal funds rate 1972–2006
Source: Federal Reserve Bank of St. Louis FRED database

current account deficit of Brady countries declined to about negative 5 percent of GDP by 1982. Similarly, this flow decline was matched by a fall in the NIIPs of Brady countries to negative 50 percent of GDP by the late 1980s (see Figure 7). Much of this change in the NIIP of Brady countries followed from both valuation effects (due to exchange rate depreciations in the early 1980s) and current account deficits (see Figure 8). By the late 1980s, current account deficits had stabilized, but valuation effects still contributed to declining NIIPs prior to the resumption of capital flows and broad resolution of the region's debt crises beginning in earnest in the 1990s. Similarly, real GDP growth in Brady countries outpaced the United States' growth rate in the 1970s, with a reversal in the early 1980s (see Figure 9). The combination of declining capital flows, lower commodity prices, rising external imbalances, and a growth slowdown created debt sustainability challenges for many Latin American countries.

3.2 The 1980s and the Baker Plan: Rescheduling, Adjustment, and Reforms

In 1982, Mexico and Brazil indicated that they could no longer honor their external obligations and entered a protracted period of macroeconomic stagnation and debt distress. Unemployment rose and wages stagnated, with the region's

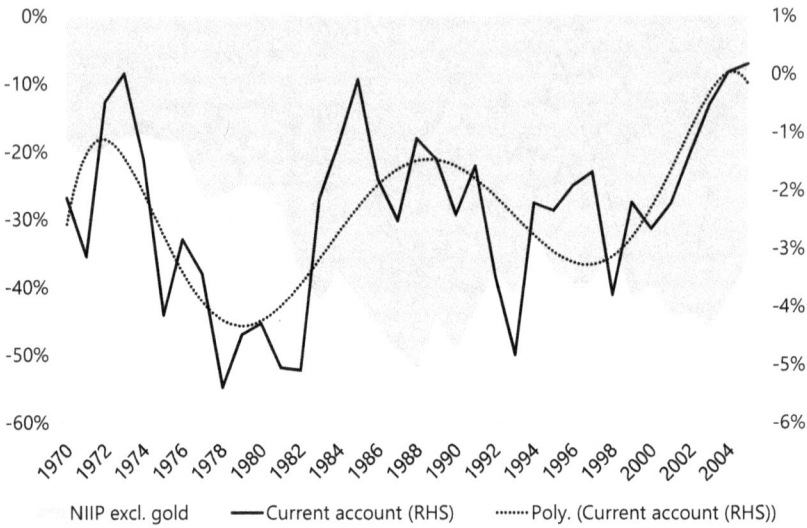

Figure 7 NIIP and current account balances of Brady countries (1970–2006)
Source: EWN database; trend line is sixth-order polynomial

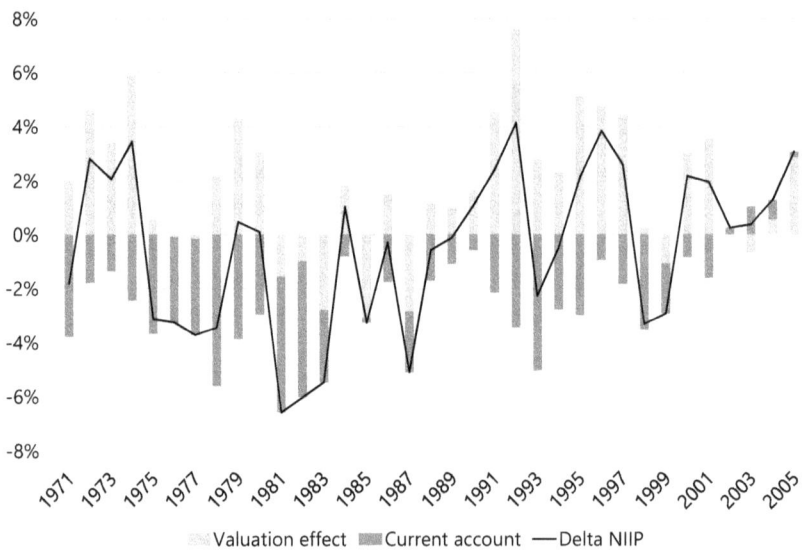

Figure 8 Change in the NIIPs of Brady countries (1981–2006)
Source: EWN Database

average per capita GDP falling over 8 percent during the 1980s, leading the United Nations to declare these years a "lost decade" for Latin America (Skidmore, Smith, & Green, 2010, p. 368), (Ocampo, 2017, p. 33).

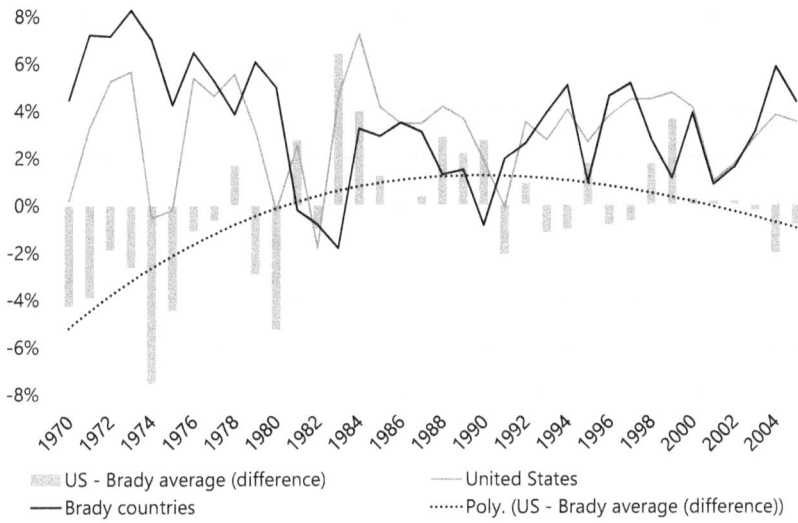

Figure 9 Real GDP growth rates: the United States versus Brady countries (1970–2006)

Source: Penn World Tables; trend line is third-order polynomial

Latin America's debt troubles were originally treated as a liquidity – rather than a solvency – problem by creditors. During the initial phase of the 1980s Latin American debt crisis, international lenders and IFIs expected that macroeconomic adjustment policies could help these countries restore sustainability and regain market access. Debtors adopted multiyear rescheduling agreements (MYRAs) to continue to service interest payments on existing debt while rescheduling principal payments coming due. The total face value of Latin America's external debt stocks was thus left unchanged during this liquidity-oriented period of the Latin American debt crisis. However, the lack of growth and new private sector lending indicated that these initial strategies were not working, and that the NPV reduction provided by MYRAs was insufficient to restore sustainability.

Thus, US Treasury Secretary James Baker developed the Baker Plan in 1985, which emphasized long-term structural reforms, rather than short-term macroeconomic adjustment. The Baker Plan proposed to adopt a case-by-case approach to liquidity challenges facing distressed Latin American countries, emphasizing the importance of sustainable macroeconomic policies as well as structural reform. Baker further called on commercial banks and IFIs to lend $30 billion in fresh capital to the fifteen countries eligible for the Baker Plan.[35]

---

[35] The list of countries in the Baker plan included Argentina, Bolivia, Brazil, Chile, Colombia, Cote d'Ivoire, Ecuador, Mexico, Morocco, Nigeria, Peru, the Philippines, Uruguay, Venezuela, and Yugoslavia. These countries were selected as they were the ones for which commercial banks

Again, face value reduction was not pursued (Sturzenegger & Zettelmeyer, 2006; Truman, 2020).

Several authors claimed that face value reductions were not seriously pursued during the Baker period due to bank capital adequacy concerns surrounding US commercial banks. During the initial phase of the Latin American debt crisis, there was a worry that defaults would lead to capitalization problems for the region's lenders. As argued by Manuel Monteagudo, US banks had major exposures to Latin American sovereigns during the Baker period and used this time to rebuild reserves and capital as distressed sovereigns continued to service their debt while undertaking macroeconomic reform. Based on an analysis of bank capital and lending decisions, Monteagudo found that more vulnerable banks were generally more reluctant to realize losses on their sovereign lending and thus were more eager to extend new financing to enable continued debt service payments from borrowers in debt distress. Partly because of the Baker Plan, banks had time to rebuild their capital positions, with loan-loss reserves nearly tripling from 1977 to 1986. This improvement in bank capital adequacy made commercial banks more prepared to handle principal write-downs while also enhancing banks' bargaining power (Monteagudo, 1994). In short, initial debt restructurings and IFI assistance, coupled with adjustment programs, helped distressed sovereigns service their debts and gave time for lenders to rebuild their buffers.

By the late 1980s, however, it was clear that face value reductions of existing loans was needed to restore debt sustainability. Several trends and complementary efforts combined to lower the reluctance of creditors and IFIs to push for debt relief. By end-1988, major commercial banks reduced their exposure to Latin America's troubled sovereigns by nearly 50 percent. Moreover, as more banks recognized the reduced market value of their claims on distressed sovereigns, they were more inclined to provide debt relief. Many debtors also made efforts to retire their external debt as well. Together, systemic stability concerns had declined by the late 1980s, though the region remained constrained by low growth, limited new lending, and unsustainable debt loads. Indeed, it was likely apparent to both debtors and creditors alike that a decade of adjustment had allowed the distressed sovereigns to make their creditors whole but not materially altered their debt trajectories and that there were limits on fiscal adjustment, hence opening the door for solvency relief. These factors combined to relax the constraints on a more fulsome debt relief process (Clark, 1994).

---

had large exposures, see (Clark, 1994). For more on the original Baker Plan, see also (Bogdanowicz-Bindert, 1986).

3.3 The Brady Plan

In March 1989, US Treasury Secretary Nicholas Brady announced a plan for reducing the debts of heavily indebted EMs. The plan proposed to offer debt relief in the form of face value reductions, face value preservation but lower coupon payments and a maturity extension, or creditors putting in new money via voluntary exchanges (see Appendix). The new debt would contain lower interest and principal payments with various inducements such as credit enhancements to encourage creditor participation in the restructuring process. These credit enhancements included using IFI funds to purchase and provide collateral for the restructured bonds, usually in the form of zero-coupon US Treasury securities, as well as macroeconomic stabilization and reform programs anchored by IMF programs and World Bank engagement to strengthen debtors' capacity to repay creditors.[36,37] The IMF's Executive Board also introduced its lending into arrears policy to allow debtors to run temporary arrears (or selective defaults) to private creditors as long as debtors were negotiating for debt relief with their existing creditors. This policy enhanced the traction of prospective Brady deals since it mitigated delays to restructurings and to IMF support. Furthermore, official sector interlocutors urged commercial banks to waive negative pledge clauses (NPCs) – or conditions that prohibit issuing new collateralized debt unless incumbent debt holders are given equivalent amounts of collateral – on the old debt. The goal of these policies was to restore debt sustainability, provide a credible plan for macroeconomic reform via IMF programs, and employ sufficient carrots and sticks to urge participation in debt treatments (Clark, 1994; Sturzenegger & Zettelmeyer, 2006; Truman, 2020).

In all seventeen countries undertook Brady restructurings beginning in 1990 through 1998 (Table 1 and Figure 10). The first Brady restructuring took place in February 1990 with Mexico, which ultimately restructured about $54 billion

---

[36] Under Brady restructurings, debtors would receive debt relief in exchange for undertaking economic reforms anchored by IMF programs. Reforms generally focused on lowering inflation, current and capital account liberalization (including reducing trade barriers), and structural reforms. See (Cline, 1995) for a summary. Recent research suggests that when countries are in debt distress, fiscal consolidation and debt relief combined produce the best outcomes for reducing long-term debt ratios. Often, such consolidations can be targeted via IMF-supported programs with UCT-quality conditionality. See (IMF, 2023a).

[37] The use of zero-coupon bonds to ensure repayment was originally devised in the US government's response to get capital into the Federal Savings and Loan Insurance Corporation to wind down troubled saving and loan banks. Given the overlap of the major bureaucratic players in devising the response to the savings and loan crisis and Baker/Brady plans, it is likely this use of zero-coupon structures in Brady restructurings drew some influence from their successful deployment during the savings and loan crisis a few years prior. For more, see (Rojas-Suárez & Weisbrod, 1996).

Table 1 Brady restructurings

Brady Country	Date of Restructuring	Debt Restructured (USD millions)	Debt Restructured (% of GDP)	Face Value Reduction	Time to Settlement (Months)
Mexico	Feb 1990	54,300	18.7	13%	14
Costa Rica	May 1990	1,384	24.1	47%	49
Venezuela	Dec 1990	19,585	40.5	7%	23
Uruguay	Jan 1991	1,610	12.0	16%	19
Nigeria	Dec 1991	5,883	9.8	35%	31
Philippines	Dec 1992	4,471	7.4	13%	29
Argentina	Apr 1993	28,476	10.8	10%	64
Jordan	Dec 1993	1,289	23.0	29%	60
Brazil	Apr 1994	43,257	7.9	9%	59
Bulgaria	Jun 1994	7,910	81.4	31%	53
Dom. Rep.	Aug 1994	1,087	7.4	40%	88
Poland	Oct 1994	13,531	13.0	32%	62
Ecuador	Feb 1995	7,170	31.2	16%	104
Panama	Apr 1996	3,936	39.2	1%	90
Peru	Mar 1997	10,600	18.8	34%	155
Vietnam	Dec 1997	782	2.3	26%	194
Cote d'Ivoire	Mar 1998	6,462	37.1	60%	180

Note: Asonuma & Trebesch (2016), Cruces & Trebesch (2013), and authors' calculations. GDP data from World Economic Outlook. Note that Russia also had a Brady-like restructuring in 1998 but was not an original Brady Plan country.

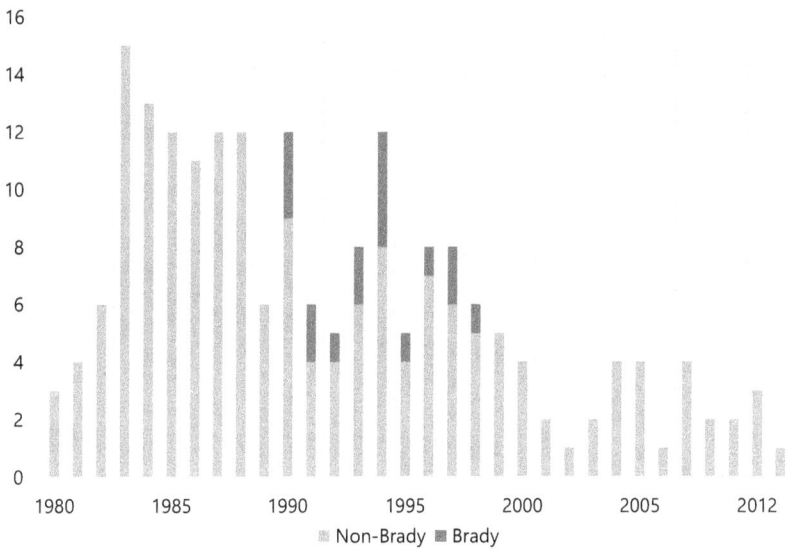

Figure 10 Number of restructurings by year (1980–2013)
Source: Asonuma & Trebesch (2016), Cruces & Trebesch (2014), and authors' calculations

of debt (worth about 19 percent of Mexico's 1990 GDP) and included a 13 percent face value reduction. The average face value reduction of all Brady restructurers was about 22 percent of GDP worth of restructured debt (Asonuma & Trebesch, 2016). Many of the early Brady restructurers, including Mexico, Nigeria, and Venezuela, were oil exporters originally targeted for structural adjustment under the preceding Baker Plan. Debt restructurings under the Brady Plan tended to take longer than other restructurings, with an average time to settlement of about six years, which is longer than the average duration of debt restructurings from 1978 to 2020 of about three years (Asonuma & Trebesch, 2016).

Brady exchanges had several features. Restructurings were done on a case-by-case basis. Debtors and creditors negotiated debt relief packages among a menu of options tailored to each restructuring request (see Table 10). In practice, the primary two options pursued via Brady exchanges were par bond exchanges and discount bond exchanges. Both restructuring options included an up-front cash payment, usually between 7 and 13 percent of the principal and interest payments of the original debt, while the remaining new obligations were securitized and restructured according to the respective exchange's features. In par bond exchanges, the face value of the new bonds was the same as the old bonds, while the new bonds would have lower fixed interest rate

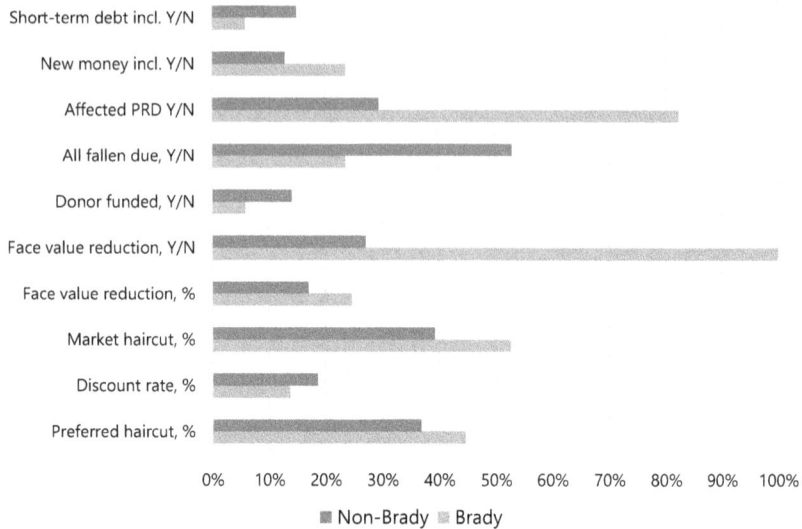

Figure 11 Characteristics of Brady restructurings

Source: Asonuma & Trebesch (2016), Cruces & Trebesch (2014), and authors' calculations

payments. Discount bonds involved face value reductions of about 30–35 percent, with variable interest rate structures (EMTA, 2022) (see Appendix). Relative to non-Brady debt restructurings that involved commercial creditors, Brady exchanges were more likely to include new money, affect principal coming due, and include larger haircuts (see Figure 11).[38]

Brady bonds included credit and liquidity enhancements to improve their attractiveness to creditors. Principal payments were collateralized by zero-coupon US Treasury securities, while interest payments were secured by high-grade investment securities purchased with IMF program augmentation and set asides that were earmarked for these debt operations.[39] To support these set asides, the IMF adopted a Debt and Debt Service Reduction (DDSR) Policy in 1989. This policy helped debtors finance the up-front costs of debt and debt service reduction operations (DDSROs), with set asides in debtors' access to IMF financing set at about 25 percent of their total access with options for

---

[38] This dataset includes defaults on commercial creditors and does not include Paris Club treatments.

[39] For a description of the US Treasury's role in providing zero-coupon securities for collateral for Brady bonds, see the August 1990 testimony of US Treasury official Allan Mendelowitz before the Committee on Banking, Finance and Urban Affairs at the US House of Representatives (Mendelowitz, 1990). At the time, the pricing decision of the zero-coupon bonds was scrutinized. For a summary of the debate, see (United Press International, 1990),

augmentation. The DDSR policy was part of a broader set of IMF policy reforms in 1989, adopted in the context of the Brady Plan, aimed at resolving the EM debt crisis by facilitating market-based restructurings and encouraging broad private creditor participation. Under the policy, the Fund provided financial support to DDSROs on eleven occasions between 1989 and 1998 (International Monetary Fund, 2021a). Debtors used DDSR support to collateralize the interest and principal of their restructured claims while also providing support for cash downpayments for debt buybacks. Zero-coupon structures offered by the Brady Plan were particularly appealing in the context of the 1980s and 1990s interest rate environment, where zero-coupon securities could be purchased at a deep discount relative to regular coupon-bearing structures given the former's higher duration (or interest rate sensitivity). Rolling interest rate guarantees – enabled by IFI lending and additional bilateral new money held in a trust at the Federal Reserve – also alleviated near-term default concerns. Together, these credit enhancements helped induce private sector involvement (PSI) in Brady restructurings.[40]

Brady bonds also had liquidity enhancements as commercial creditors were able to turn their claims into tradable financial securities. Indeed, one of the benefits of the Brady Plan was to offer the opportunity to bilateral creditors to turn illiquid loans into tradable securities, thereby strengthening the liquidity of restructured claims while reducing creditor concentration (Miles, 1999).[41] There is also evidence that Brady bonds tended to have a higher price (and thus a lower exit yield) compared to non-Brady restructured claims, indicating that the collateralization and liquidity enhancements of Brady bonds reduced market perceptions of debtors' post-restructuring risk premium (IMF, 2021a). Brady bonds helped open new categories of institutional investors that were attracted to the relatively higher returns offered by Brady bonds while taking advantage of the safety provided by their collateralized structure. This benefit is evidenced by the fact that external sovereign bonds generally offer excess returns over the implied needed compensation for the risk of default, while

---

[40] As discussed by IMF (2021a), the potential benefit offered by using these financial carrots, including achieving larger face value write-downs via restructurings, need to be weighed against the cost of providing them. Potential risks and opportunity costs of DDSROs include ensuring adequate private sector participation in the post-restructured debt pool to provide an adequate margin of safety for preferred creditors should debtors face additional stress. Moreover, the announcement of market-based buybacks could raise the price of debt in the secondary market, thereby reducing some of the savings available to debtors from debt buy-backs facilitated in part by DDSROs.

[41] Of course, creditors may need to overcome domestic legal constraints that would hamper their willingness to convert existing bilateral loans into tradable bonds, such as obtaining parliamentary approval.

the same may not necessarily be true for bilateral claims (Meyer, Reinhart, & Trebesch, 2022).

For their part, Brady countries undertook significant macroeconomic and structural reforms. These reforms included measures under IMF programs and structural reforms encouraged by the World Bank, among others. These programs served two purposes: They enhanced the capacity to repay restructured claims while signaling debtors' commitment to reform and sound public finances. Brady Plan era reforms often followed several years' worth of macroeconomic adjustment programs undertaken during the MYRA and Baker Plan eras.

The Brady Plan had strong ownership by the United States. In the 1980s, the United States in close collaboration with Japan underwrote the Brady Plan by providing enhancements for interest and principal payments on the restructured bonds. The US government used its influence at the IFIs, as well as its connections to its commercial creditors, to urge debt relief via Brady exchanges. While not documented in the literature, it is plausible that senior US Treasury leadership – many of whom had deep ties to commercial lenders – encouraged commercial creditor participation via moral suasion. More broadly, the United States took a leadership role in helping to address the challenges of engaging multiple stakeholders in debt restructuring, including by helping restructurers navigate the stigma and operational opacity associated with debt restructuring. Additionally, the United States provided leadership to the IFIs to build a consensus to support implementation of the plan.[42]

3.4 Summary

This section provided historical context for the Brady Plan, detailing the evolution of global capital markets from the end of World War II through the Bretton Woods period and into the era of capital mobility. The original Bretton Woods system facilitated trade liberalization and stable global finance until the late 1960s when the US balance of payments swung into deficit, leading to the development of Eurodollar and eurocurrency markets. It highlighted the role of global banks in allocating capital to EM countries and the impact of the Volcker shock in the early 1980s, which led to severe capital flow reversals and debt distress in many Latin American and other EM countries. Initially, the global response to these crises treated them as liquidity problems rather than solvency issues, including via MYRAs. The Baker Plan was introduced in 1985,

---

[42] The United States paved the way to debt relief by urging its commercial creditors to waive NPCs, for instance, when engaging in Brady exchanges. For more on the US role in the Brady Plan, see (Clark, 1994).

emphasizing long-term structural reforms and fresh capital to distressed countries. Despite these efforts, face value reductions were not pursued due to concerns about bank capital adequacy. By the late 1980s, it became clear that debt relief was necessary, leading US Treasury Secretary Nicholas Brady to introduce the Brady Plan in 1989. This plan aimed to provide debt relief through face value reductions, lower coupon payments, maturity extensions, and new money via voluntary exchanges, supported by credit enhancements such as zero-coupon US Treasury securities and IFI-supported adjustment programs. The Brady Plan involved case-by-case debt restructurings with options for par bond exchanges and discount bond exchanges, supported by credit and liquidity enhancements. Having described the historical background and details about the Brady Plan, this Element now turns to its main empirical analysis of the impact of the Brady Plan on the macroeconomic outcomes of Brady restructurers.

4 Analyzing the Macroeconomic Impact of the Brady Plan

This section provides the main empirical analysis of this Element to analyze the macroeconomic impact of the original Brady Plan. To distinguish the effect of debt relief from that of common shocks, macroeconomic outcomes for Brady countries are compared with a similar group of forty EMDEs that did not receive debt relief under the Brady Plan. In so doing, this Element's research design addresses the nonrandom nature of achieving debt relief treatment by using DiD and SCM to compare the outcomes of Brady restructurings with otherwise observationally similar countries.[43] This section details the empirical strategy and presents the results from this analysis.

4.1 Sample and Sources

The sample for this Element's empirical analysis includes ten Brady countries for which sufficient data could be obtained. These countries included Argentina, Brazil, Costa Rica, Dominican Republic, Ecuador, Jordan, Mexico, Nigeria, Peru, and the Philippines.[44] Data sources are presented in Table 2. The control

---

[43] Recent applications of synthetic control methods include studies on the macroeconomic impacts of economic liberalization episodes (Nannicini & Billmeier, 2011) and (Billmeier & Nannicini, 2013); structural and tax reforms (Newiak & Willems, 2017), (Adhikari et al., 2016), and (Adhikari & Alm, 2016); the recent Debt Service Suspension Initiative (Lang, Mihalyi, & Presbitero); IMF precautionary lending programs and rescue loans (Essers & Ide, 2019) and (Kuruc, 2022), respectively; and Brexit (Born et al., 2019).

[44] The sample does not include Brady cases of Bulgaria, Cote d'Ivoire, Panama, Poland, Uruguay, Venezuela, and Vietnam due to incomplete data. Note that Russia had a Brady-like deal in 1998 but was not an original Brady Plan nor Baker Plan country, and hence was omitted from this Element's analysis.

Table 2 Variables and data sources

Variable	Source(s)
Gross government debt	Global Debt Database (Mbaye, Moreno Badia, & Chae, 2018), Historical Public Debt Database, World Economic Outlook
External debt	World Bank Development Indicators
Real GDP	Penn World Table 10.0 (Feenstra, Inklaar, & Timmer, 2015)
GDP deflator	World Economic Outlook and World Bank Development Indicators
Trade openness	Penn World Table 10.0 (Feenstra, Inklaar, & Timmer, 2015)
FDI stock, external liabilities	External Wealth of Nations (Lane & Milesi-Ferretti, 2018)
Physical capital stock Human capital index Employment Population Labor income share	Penn World Table 10.0 (Feenstra, Inklaar, & Timmer, 2015)

Note: Any potential biases or omissions in data sources could impact the paper's results. The use of multiple methods and robustness checks helps reduce, but not eliminate, the risks associated with issues from data coverage.

group consists of seventeen countries that received debt restructuring between 1970 and 2013 but did not sign Brady deals and twenty-three other EMDEs that did not seek debt treatments (see Table 3). Summary statistics of the main macroeconomic variables under consideration are reported in Table 4.

4.2 Methodology

A DiD regression was run to assess the impact of Brady restructurings on various variables of interest (see Table 3).[45] The proposed specification is described in equation (3):

$$y_{it} = \beta \cdot brady_i \times post_t + \gamma_i + \gamma_t + \epsilon_{it}, \tag{3}$$

where $post_t$ is a dummy equal to 1 in 1999, and equal to zero in 1989. $brady_i$ is a dummy equal to 1 for Brady countries. γ_i and γ_t are country- and year-specific fixed effects. Coefficient β captures the impact of the Brady restructuring – that

---
[45] For a background on the DiD approach, see (Baker, Larcker, & Wang, 2021).

Table 3 Sample of countries

Brady (10)	Non-Brady Restructurings (17)	Non-Brady Non-Restructurings (23)
Argentina*	Bolivia	Bangladesh
Brazil	Cameroon	Benin
Costa Rica	Congo, Rep.	Botswana
Dominican Republic	Gabon	Burundi
Ecuador*	Honduras	Colombia
Jordan*	Jamaica	Egypt, Arab Rep.
Mexico	Kenya	El Salvador
Nigeria*	Madagascar	Eswatini
Peru	Malawi	Fiji
Philippines	Morocco	Ghana
	Niger	Guatemala
	Pakistan	Haiti
	Paraguay	India
	Senegal	Indonesia
	Sierra Leone	Iran, Islamic Rep.
	Togo	Lesotho
	Türkiye	Mali
		Mauritius
		Myanmar
		Nepal
		Sri Lanka
		Thailand
		Tunisia

Note: Table lists EMDEs included in the full sample for the DiD analysis. The sample excludes Brady cases Bulgaria, Cote d'Ivoire, Poland, Uruguay, Venezuela, and Vietnam due to incomplete data.
* denotes oil exporter

is, it captures the difference in the outcome variable y_{it} for Brady countries relative to the pre-Brady period and non-Brady countries. Note that both average treatments (with an event study at 1989) and a staggered treatment (to accommodate the timing of when Brady restructurings took place in each treated country) are used.

As an additional check, an SCM was used. The SCM provides a useful analytical tool to assess the impact of treatment (in this case, a Brady restructuring) on a country relative to a *synthetic control*, or a combination of

Table 4 Selected summary statistics

Variable	Measure	Brady	Non-Brady Restructurings	Non-Brady Non-Restructurings
Gross government debt, % of GDP, 1989	Mean	70.7	71.1	56.7
	Median	58.9	53.9	48.8
Gross government debt, % of GDP, 1999	Mean	55.4	73.9	54.6
	Median	48.3	63.4	44.3
External debt, % of GDP, 1989	Mean	77.9	81.1	60.8
	Median	75.2	80	43.2
External debt, % of GDP, 1999	Mean	54.9	89.5	52.7
	Median	51.3	68.3	40.4
Real GDP growth, %, 1985–1989 av.	Mean	2.8	2.7	4.5
	Median	2.4	3.1	4.6
Real GDP growth, %, 1990–1999 av.	Mean	3.4	1.9	4.6
	Median	3.4	2.3	4.8
Inflation %, 1985–1989 av.	Mean	220	163	11
	Median	21.2	6.1	10
Inflation %, 1990–1999 av.	Mean	186	18.3	12.7
	Median	21.7	10	10.2
Trade openness, 1989	Mean	21.5	28.5	25.2
	Median	17.2	18.1	15.3

Trade openness, 1999	Mean	39.7	34.9	31.5
	Median	36.8	20.4	20.4
FDI stock, share of external liabilities, 1989	Mean	12.3	10.7	18.9
	Median	10.3	8.6	13.4
FDI stock, share of external liabilities, 1999	Mean	26.1	15.8	24.5
	Median	27.6	14.1	20.3
Current account, % of GDP, 1985–1989 av.	Mean	-2.4	-5.2	-0.3
	Median	-2	-4.6	-2.2
Current account, % of GDP, 1990–1999 av.	Mean	-2.9	-5	-3.1
	Median	-2.8	-4.6	-2.3
Net investment income, % of GDP, 1985–1989	Mean	-5.2	-4.7	-3
	Median	-4.9	-3.9	-2.3
Net investment income, % of GDP, 1985–1989	Mean	-3.5	-4.8	-1.6
	Median	-3.7	-3.1	-1.5

Source: Authors' calculations

comparator countries.[46] This study is interested in the effect α_{it} of the Brady Plan on macro outcome y_{it} in country i at time $t \geq t_0$, where t_0 is the time period when the Brady Plan starts to impact the outcome. This effect can be stated as per equation (4):

$$\alpha_{it} = y_{it}^I - y_{it}^N, \tag{4}$$

where y_{it}^I is the value of y_{it} when the Brady Plan takes place, and y_{it}^N is the value of y_{it} in the absence of the Brady Plan. y_{it}^I is observed, whereas y_{it}^N is not. The SCM estimates a counterfactual (i.e., the synthetic control) for y_{it}^N using a weighted average of the observations from the control group (the comparator pool) such that

$$\hat{y}_{it}^N = \sum_{n \neq i} w_n y_{nt}, \tag{5}$$

where the weights w_n are constructed such that the synthetic control dependent variable matches pretreatment characteristics of the treated country as closely as possible. Specifically, the vector of weights solves equation (6):

$$\min_W \|X_1 - X_0 W\|_V = \sqrt{(X_1 - X_0 W)' V (X_1 - X_0 W)} \tag{6}$$

subject to $w_n \geq 0 \forall n \neq i$

$$\sum_{n \neq i} w_n = 1,$$

where V is a symmetric and positive semi-definite matrix that weighs the importance of pretreatment characteristics, constructed to minimize the mean-squared prediction error for the level of the outcome variable (e.g., external debt to GDP) in the pretreatment periods (1981–89). As an example, Table 5 includes the weights of the synthetic controls for gross public debt. After obtaining the weights, the treatment effect of the Brady Plan at time t is constructed as per equation (7):

$$\hat{\alpha}_{it} = y_{it}^I - \hat{y}_{it}^N. \tag{7}$$

To assess the macroeconomic impact of the Brady Plan, decompositions of growth and debt dynamics are calculated. For real GDP growth, Cobb–Douglas production functions of real GDP with physical capital and effective labor as

---

[46] (Abadie & Gardeazabal, 2003) developed the SCM, which was subsequently extended by (Abadie, Diamond, & Hainmueller, 2010). For more detailed discussions of the SCM in a macro context, see (Newiak & Willems, 2017) and (Kuruc, 2022).

Table 5 Country weights of synthetic controls for gross public debt

Brady Country	Argentina	Brazil	Costa Rica	Dominican Republic	Ecuador	Jordan	Mexico	Nigeria	Peru	Philippines
Control										
Bangladesh	0	0	0	0	0.547	0	0	0.281	0	0
Benin	0.518	0	0	0	0	0	0	0	0.274	0
Bolivia	0	0	0	0	0	0	0	0	0	0
Botswana	0	0	0	0	0	0	0	0	0.141	0
Burundi	0	0	0.624	0	0	0	0	0	0.519	0
Cameroon	0	0	0.335	0	0	0	0	0	0	0
Colombia	0.053	0	0	0	0	0.121	0	0	0	0
Congo, Rep.	0	0	0	0	0	0	0	0	0	0
Egypt, Arab Rep.	0	0	0.042	0	0	0	0	0	0	0
El Salvador	0	0	0	0	0	0	0	0	0	0
Eswatini	0	0.161	0	0	0	0	0.134	0.154	0	0
Fiji	0	0	0	0	0	0	0	0.362	0	0
Gabon	0	0	0	0	0	0	0	0	0.009	0
Ghana	0	0	0	0	0	0	0	0	0.058	0
Guatemala	0.266	0	0	0	0.009	0	0	0.204	0	0
Haiti	0	0	0	0	0	0	0.006	0	0	0.418
Honduras	0	0	0	0	0	0	0	0	0	0
India	0	0.048	0	0	0	0	0.236	0	0	0
Indonesia	0	0.196	0	0	0	0	0	0	0	0

Table 5 (cont.)

Brady Country	Argentina	Brazil	Costa Rica	Dominican Republic	Ecuador	Jordan	Mexico	Nigeria	Peru	Philippines
Iran, Islamic Rep.	0	0	0	0	0	0	0	0	0	0
Jamaica	0	0	0	0	0	0	0	0	0	0
Kenya	0	0	0	0.005	0	0	0	0	0	0
Lesotho	0	0	0	0	0	0	0	0	0	0
Madagascar	0	0	0	0.363	0.091	0	0	0	0	0.198
Malawi	0	0	0	0	0	0	0	0	0	0
Mali	0.13	0	0	0	0.352	0	0	0	0	0
Mauritius	0	0	0	0	0	0.879	0	0	0	0
Morocco	0	0	0	0	0	0	0	0	0	0
Myanmar	0	0	0	0	0	0	0	0	0	0
Nepal	0	0	0	0	0	0	0	0	0	0
Niger	0	0	0	0	0	0	0	0	0	0
Pakistan	0	0	0	0.632	0	0	0	0	0	0
Paraguay	0	0	0	0	0	0	0	0	0	0
Senegal	0	0	0	0	0	0	0.086	0	0	0.006
Sierra Leone	0.032	0	0	0	0	0	0	0	0	0.238
Sri Lanka	0	0	0	0	0	0	0.485	0	0	0
Thailand	0	0	0	0	0	0	0	0	0	0
Togo	0	0.595	0	0	0	0	0.051	0	0	0.14
Tunisia	0	0	0	0	0	0	0	0	0	0
Turkiye	0	0	0	0	0	0	0	0	0	0

Source: Authors' calculations

inputs is specified as per equation (8). The growth rate of real GDP can be decomposed in first differences as per equation (8):

$$\Delta \ln Y_t = \Delta \ln TFP_t + \frac{\alpha}{1-\alpha} \Delta \ln k_t + \Delta \ln h_t + \Delta \ln\left(\frac{L_t}{P_t}\right) + \Delta \ln P_t, \quad (8)$$

where Y_t is real GDP, TFP_t is total factor factor productivity, k_t is capital per unit of output, h_t is a country's human capital index, $\frac{L_t}{P_t}$ is the employment to population ratio, and P_t is population. α is the capital share, which is measured as 1 minus the labor share in Penn World Table 10.0.

The change in the debt-to-GDP ratio can be decomposed into the contributions from debt relief, economic growth, and a residual. This change is decomposed as per equation (9):

$$d_t - d_{t-1} = -relief_t - \frac{g_t}{1+g_t} d_{t-1} + o_t, \quad (9)$$

where d_t is gross government debt to GDP, $relief_t$ is debt relief to GDP, g_t is the growth rate of real GDP, and o_t is the residual that captures the primary balance, exchange rate and inflation effects, and stock-flow adjustments. To assess the contribution of higher output growth of Brady countries to changes in the debt to GDP ratio, the exercise iterates forward from 1989 using a counterfactual growth rate that is two percentage points lower than the observed growth rate. Note that two percentage points equals the magnitude of the uptick in trend growth of Brady countries in 1990–99 relative to 1980–89.

The benefit of this research design is employing several methods to assess the impact of Brady treatments on the macroeconomic outcomes of Brady restructurers. Each method has methodological benefits and costs, which are compensated by employing other methods and analyzing the results holistically. The baseline DiD is simple and transparent. Its lack of a staggered treatment means that it is more robust to the concern that there might be spillover effects on later treatments from earlier treatments. Hence, the baseline DiD assesses the average treatment effect of the Brady group regardless of when the treatment occurred (i.e., it is time-independent). However, one drawback of this approach is that it assumes parallel trends and that the parallel trend assumption may be violated. Moreover, the baseline DiD may understate the treatment effects in the absence of spillovers. Both the SCM and staggered DiD compensate for these concerns. The SCM directly addresses the parallel trends assumption because it constructs a control group that by design fully matches the pre-trend of the treated group. The drawback of the SCM is that its results can be sensitive to the choice of comparators included in deriving the comparator synthetic control. They also assume unobserved confounders are time-invariant, that is, are constant throughout the period of analysis. The staggered DiD considers the heterogeneity of the timing of the treatment, thus avoids some of the issues related to assuming parallel trends present in the baseline DiD results, but restructurings in the early-treated group could directly affect outcomes in later-treated countries, biasing estimated effects.

4.3 Results of the Standard DiD, Staggered DiD, and SCM

In the decade following the first Brady deal, public debt levels of Brady countries dropped by 20 percentage points of GDP relative to non-Brady countries. Public debt levels of Brady countries grew faster than those of the control group in the decade before 1990 (Figure 12).[47] After the first Brady deal, debt levels of Brady countries declined by about 25 percentage points of GDP, albeit from a much higher level, while debt levels of the control group flatlined. Similarly, average external debt burdens of Brady countries, which grew at similar rates to non-Brady countries before 1990, fell by roughly 25 percentage points relative to the control group in the following decade (Figure 13). These

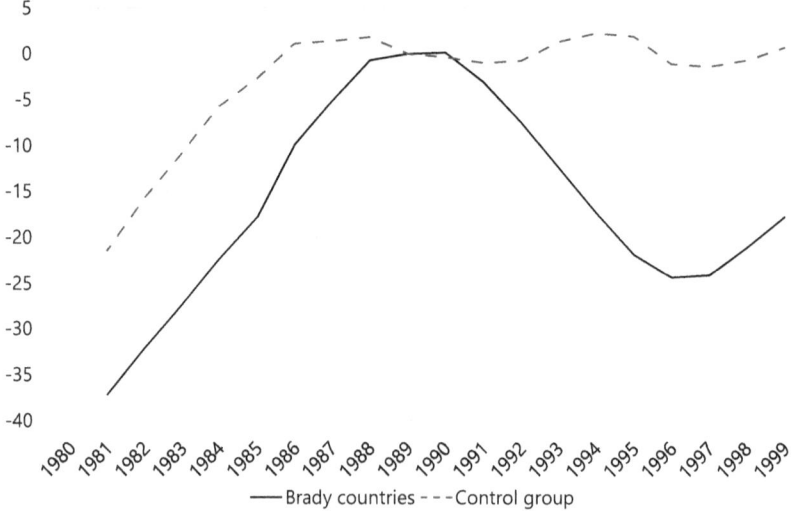

Figure 12 Evolution of public debt following the first Brady deal (% of GDP, 1989 = 0)

Source: Table 2 and authors' calculations

---

[47] Public and external debt (as a percentage of GDP) from 1980 to 1999 in a sample of ten Brady countries and fifty-three EMDEs that serve as the control group are presented in Figures 12 and 13. Lines show group averages by year relative to 1989, the year before the first Brady restructuring.

Figure 13 Evolution of external debt following the first Brady deal (1980–99, % of GDP, 1989 = 0)

Source: Table 2 and authors' calculations

findings suggest the Brady Plan had the first-order effect of bringing down debt burdens and thereby enhancing debt sustainability, in line with its goals. Tables 6 and 7 summarize the results of the DiD regressions.[48]

Brady countries caught up to the same economic growth trend as other EMDEs after their restructurings. In the decade prior to the first debt relief, real GDP of Brady countries grew at an average rate of 1.5 percent per year, whereas non-Brady countries grew at an average rate of more than 3 percent. During the decade following the first Brady deal in 1990, the growth rate of Brady countries more than doubled to 3.4 percent. Economic growth in the control group was unchanged relative to its pre-1990 growth path (Figure 14). In 1999, output of Brady countries was 26 percent higher relative to their pre-restructuring trend.

Following debt relief, inflation rates of Brady countries declined significantly relative to the control group. Inflation was high in Brady countries before the restructurings (Figure 15).[49] The mean of the annual growth rate of Brady countries' output deflator peaked at 600 percent in 1989, and the median peaked

---

[48] In conducting this analysis, the contribution of changes in fiscal stances to overall debt burden reductions was considered but not pursued due to the lack of granular fiscal data on Brady countries in the 1980s and early 1990s.

[49] This panel includes group medians because means are impacted by hyperinflationary episodes, such as in Brazil.

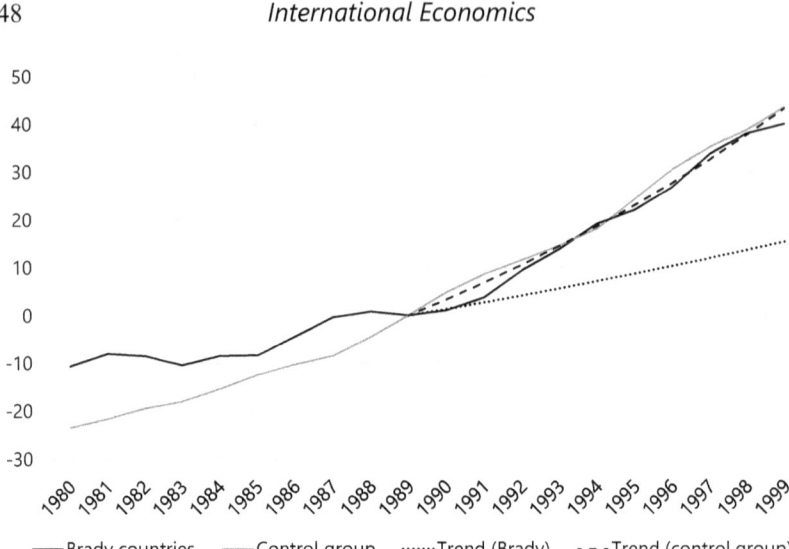

Figure 14 Evolution of real GDP following the first Brady deal (1989 = 0)
Source: Table 2 and authors' calculations

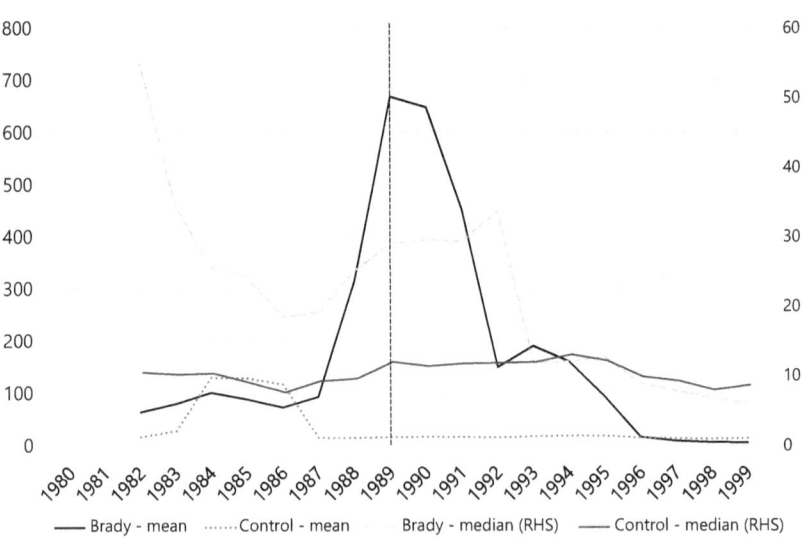

Figure 15 Inflation, three-year average
Source: Table 2 and authors' calculations

at 30 percent in 1992. Yet by 1999, both mean and median inflation rates of the Brady group had fallen to below the control group.

Figure 16 Trade openness, % of GDP (1989 = 0)
Source: Table 2 and authors' calculations

The faster growth of Brady countries was achieved through greater integration into global trade and direct investment. Trade openness of EMDEs declined in the 1980s, falling from 40 percent of GDP to less than 25 percent in 1989. Following the first Brady restructuring, openness of Brady countries increased back to 40 percent in 1990, 10 percentage points above the control group (Figure 16).[50] Brady countries also achieved greater exposure to foreign technologies by shifting a larger share of external liabilities into foreign direct investment (FDI), with the stock of FDI being as a share of all external liabilities, expressed as a percentage. Between 1989 and 1999, the share of FDI in external liabilities increased by 13 percentage points, more than double the increase relative to the control group (Figure 17).

By reducing external debt service, Brady deals increased the net resource inflow into Brady countries, providing space for imports of growth-enhancing investment goods. In the 1980s, current account deficits narrowed in EMDEs, as external inflows dried up and external debt service increased (Figure 18). After the first Brady restructuring, the path of current accounts did not diverge between Brady countries and the control group. But net investment income went up substantially in Brady countries, increasing by close to 3 percentage points of GDP in 1997 relative to 1989 (Figure 19).

---

[50] Trade openness is measured as the sum of imports and exports as a percentage of GDP.

Figure 17 FDI stock, share of external liabilities, (1989 = 0)

Source: Table 2 and authors' calculations

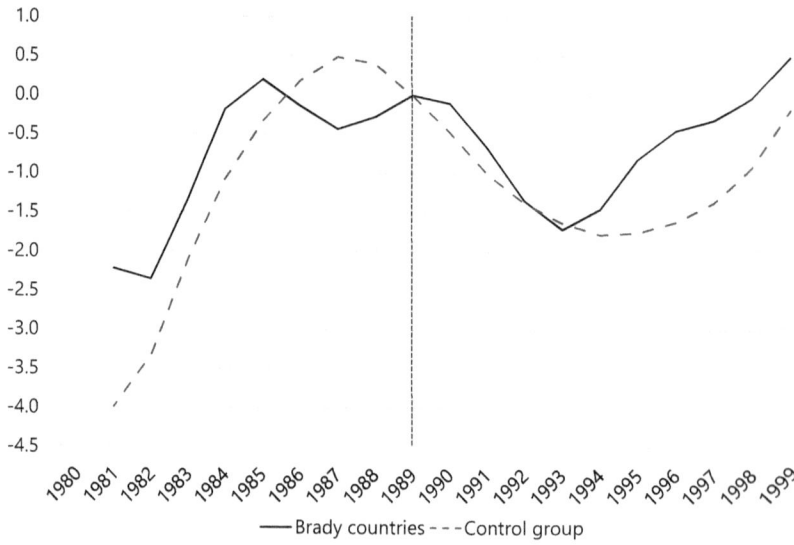

Figure 18 Current account, % of GDP (1989 = 0)

Source: Table 2 and authors' calculations

Higher TFP growth was the main driver of the pickup in economic growth following the Brady restructurings. In the 1980s, average growth of TFP was negative in Brady countries. Output growth was mainly driven by population

Figure 19 Net investment income, % of GDP (1989 = 0)
Source: Table 2 and authors' calculations

growth and output per capita stagnated. In the decade following the first Brady deal, TFP growth increased by 2.5 percentage points per year (Figure 20).[51] The pickup in market access of Brady countries, anchored by the marketability of collateralized restructured instruments and assured interest payments, may have contributed to this boost in TFP growth as well as investment, as discussed previously.[52]

Brady countries achieved better macroeconomic performance compared to both other countries that restructured during the same period and countries that did not restructure. Tables 6 and 7 show the output for separate regressions that use only other restructurings (countries that underwent a non-Brady restructuring between 1980 and 2007) and non-restructurings as control groups.

Government debt and inflation fell by similar magnitudes in Brady countries compared to both control groups. External debt fell more relative to other restructuring cases. The growth impact of the Brady Plan was largest relative to other restructurings. These findings suggest that it was the Brady Plan itself,

---

[51] Capital deepening (measured as the change in the capital to output ratio) contributed negatively to growth in Brady countries. This result may indicate that the increase in TFP growth in Brady countries was labor-biased.

[52] The pickup in market access after Brady deals is documented in Arslanalp and Henry (2005), who show that Brady countries experienced a subsequent increase in net resource transfers (net resource flows minus interest payments on long-term loans and foreign direct investment profits).

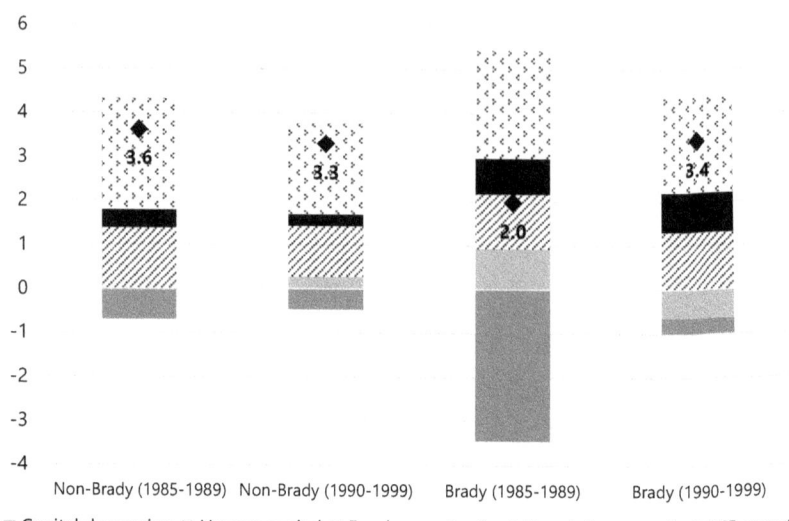

Figure 20 Growth decomposition (average contributions (1990–99 versus 1985–89)

Source: PWT and authors' calculations

and not the macroeconomic context that gave rise to the restructuring, that led to the improvement of macroeconomic fundamentals in Brady countries.

The long-term impact of the Brady restructurings on debt levels was many times greater than the face value reductions. The average face value reduction of a Brady deal was 3.3 percent of 1999 GDP. With public debt levels of Brady countries 20 percentage points lower in 1999 relative to the control group, and attributing this difference to the Brady Plan, this implies a "Brady multiplier" of about six times the initial face value reduction. More than half of this effect is accounted for by the marked increase in output growth (Figure 21).

Brady countries undertook more ambitious structural reforms than non-Brady restructurers. One of the potential explanations of higher TFP growth in Brady restructurers could relate to their successful implementation of structural reforms relative to non-Brady restructurers. Furthermore, Brady countries made more progress on product market reforms relative to non-Brady countries. Brady countries also achieved greater levels of financial deepening, as evidenced by their better performance on improving access to both domestic and external finance (see Figures 22–25). This result contrasts with the experience of some Heavily Indebted Poor Country (HIPC) restructurers, who according to one study saw a net decline in inflows from China and other emerging creditors after receiving debt relief (Cordella, Cufre, & Presbitero, 2025). Brady countries tended to meet more of their IMF program quantitative targets relative to non-Brady peers, indicating a

Panel A

Table 6 Average treatment effects, DiD regressions

Dependent Variable	Gross Government Debt to GDP, %, Three-Year Average			External Debt to GDP, %, Three-Year Average		
Control group	All EMDEs	Restructurings	Non-Restructurings	All EMDEs	Restructurings	Non-Restructurings
$brady\_i \times post\_t$	−10.2	−12.1	−8.8	−10.7	−14	−8.2
	−6.6	−7.5	−7	−8.9	−9.4	−9.8
Constant	62.9***	74.3***	54.2***	68.5***	86.1***	55.2***
	−0.08	−0.21	−0.15	−0.11	−0.26	−0.2
Country fixed effects	Y	Y	Y	Y	Y	Y
Year fixed effects	Y	Y	Y	Y	Y	Y
Observations	820	360	480	820	360	480
Countries	50	27	33	50	27	33
Adjusted R-squared	0.87	0.86	0.86	0.86	0.87	0.82

Panel B

Dependent Variable	Gross Government Debt to GDP, %, Three-Year Average			External Debt to GDP, %, Three-Year Average		
Control group	All EMDEs	Restructurings	Non-Restructurings	All EMDEs	Restructurings	Non-Restructurings
brady_i×post_t	12.6**	15.8***	10.2	-180	-179	-180
	-5.3	-5.4	-7.3	-165	-167	-166
Constant	1.0***	-3.1***	4.3***	19.3***	27.6***	20.1***
	-0.06	-0.15	-0.15	-2	-4.6	-3.5
Country fixed effects	Y	Y	Y	Y	Y	Y
Year fixed effects	Y	Y	Y	Y	Y	Y
Observations	820	360	480	820	360	480
Countries	50	27	33	50	27	33
Adjusted R-squared	0.55	0.63	0.52	0.53	0.52	0.52

Note: Table summarizes regression results from differences-in-differences regression with staggered treatment. Post period refers to the 5th year after the pre-treatment (restructuring) year. Robust standard errors clustered at the country level in parentheses. ***: significant at 1%; **: significant at 5%; *: significant at 10.

Table 7 Average treatment effects, DiD Regressions (cont.)

Panel C

Dependent Variable	Gross Government Debt to GDP, %, Three-Year Average			External Debt to GDP, %, Three-Year Average		
Control group	All EMDEs	Restructurings	Non-Restructurings	All EMDEs	Restructurings	Non-Restructurings
brady_i×post_t	−1.7	−3.2	−0.58	3.6**	3.9*	3.4*
	−3.2	−3.6	−3.3	−1.6	−2.1	−1.8
Constant	30.1***	31.3***	29.2***	17.6***	12.9***	21.1***
	−0.04	−0.1	−0.07	−0.02	−0.06	−0.04
Country fixed effects	Y	Y	Y	Y	Y	Y
Year fixed effects	Y	Y	Y	Y	Y	Y
Observations	820	360	480	820	360	480
Countries	50	27	33	50	27	33
Adjusted R-squared	0.94	0.94	0.94	0.89	0.67	0.92

Panel D

Dependent Variable	Gross Government Debt to GDP, %, Three-Year Average				External Debt to GDP, %, Three-Year Average			
Control group	All EMDEs	Restructurings	Non-Restructurings		All EMDEs	Restructurings	Non-Restructurings	
brady_i× post_t	0.92	0.87	0.96		0.67	1	0.38	
	-1.5	-1.5	-1.6		-0.6	-0.77	-0.6	
Constant	-3.7***	-4.8***	-2.8***		-3.1***	-4.7***	-1.8***	
	-0.02	-0.04	-0.04		-0.01	-0.02	-0.01	
Country fixed effects	Y	Y	Y		Y	Y	Y	
Year fixed effects	Y	Y	Y		Y	Y	Y	
Observations	820	360	480		820	360	480	
Countries	50	27	33		50	27	33	
Adjusted R-squared	0.61	0.65	0.53		0.85	0.87	0.51	

Note: The table summarizes regression results from DiD regression with staggered treatment. Post-period refers to the fifth year after the pretreatment (restructuring) year. Robust standard errors clustered at the country level in parentheses. ***: significant at 1%; **: significant at 5%; *: significant at 10.

Figure 21 Debt decomposition (average change relative to control group, 1989–99)

Source: PWT and authors' calculations

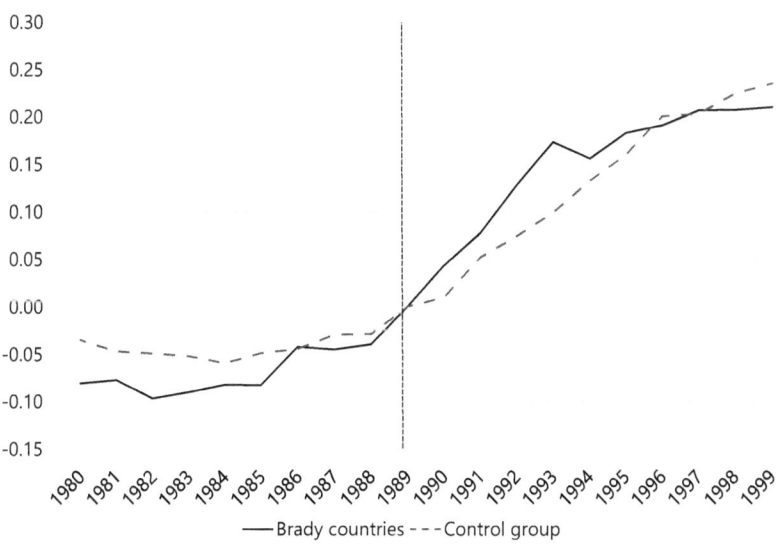

Figure 22 Trade restrictions reforms (1989 = 0)

Source: IMF Structural Reforms Database and authors' calculations

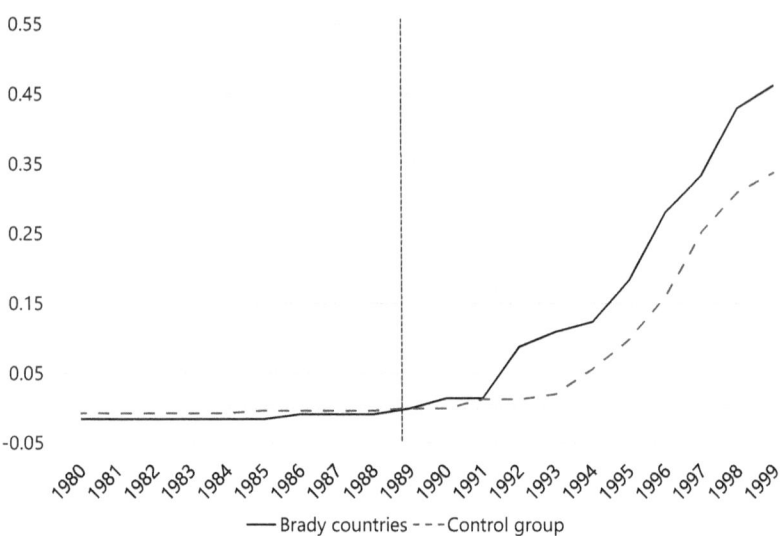

Figure 23 Product market reforms (1989 = 0)

Source: IMF Structural Reforms Database and authors' calculations

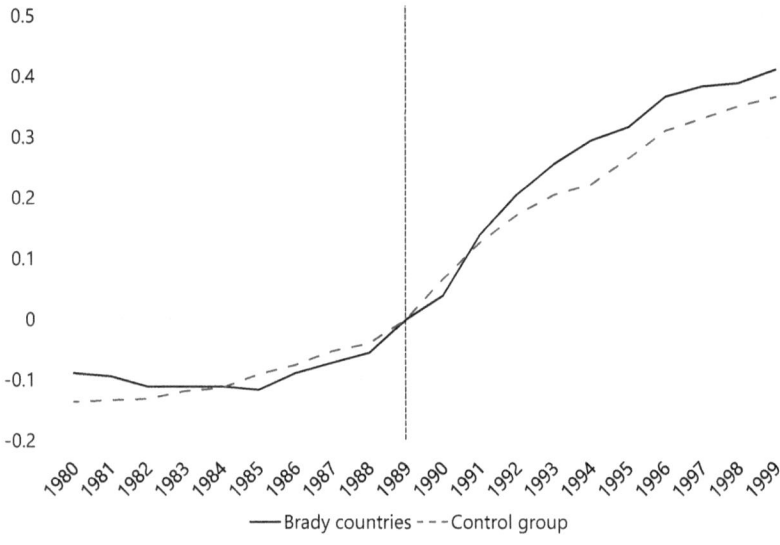

Figure 24 Domestic finance reforms (1989 = 0)

Source: IMF Structural Reforms Database and authors' calculations

generally higher quality of macroeconomic policymaking in Brady countries (see Figure 26).[53] These results would indicate that the structural reform efforts of Brady countries were greater than non-Brady countries.

---

[53] The variable in Figure 26 measures the share of quantitative performance criteria (QPC) that were either not met or for which a waiver was requested. The chart shows the average per country

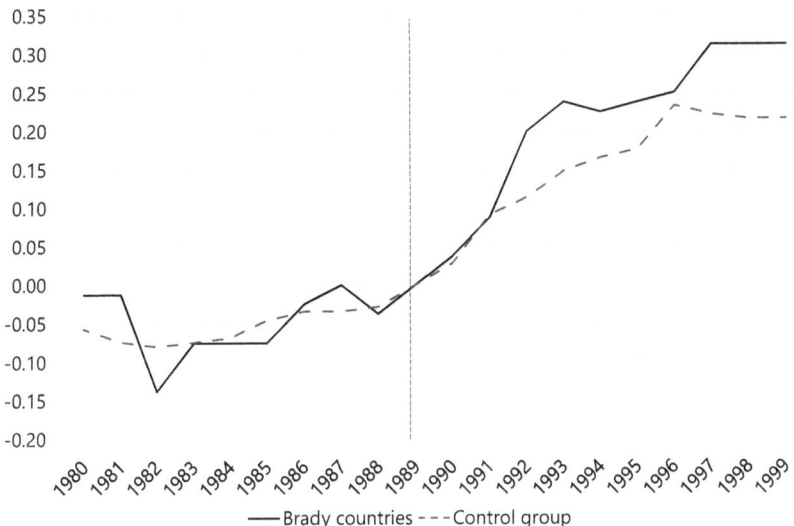

Figure 25 External finance reforms (1989 = 0)
Source: IMF Structural Reforms Database and authors' calculations

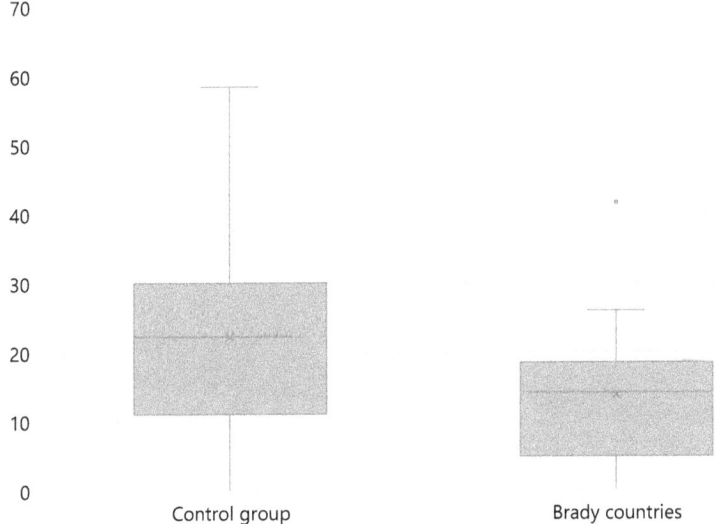

Figure 26 IMF program performance in Brady restructurers versus comparators
Source: IMF MONA database and authors' calculations

---

between 1993 and 2022. QPCs that were modified are not included. Brady country sample includes all those listed in Table 1, excluding Nigeria. Non-Brady countries include all other countries in the MONA database between 1993 and 2002.

Baseline DiD results are in line with the results of a SCM. The key assumption in the DiD method is that in the absence of treatment (a Brady restructuring) the average outcomes in both treated and control groups follow "parallel trends," that is, in the absence of treatment, the difference between Brady and non-Brady countries would be constant over time. The pre-trends in Figures 12–14 are broadly parallel.

A SCM is also employed to check the results, which confirm the results obtained in the DiD regressions (see Figures 27–33). Recall that SCMs constructed a counterfactual path of a given dependent variable based on a weighted average of comparators for which the pre-trend is the same as the treated country's dependent variable. The SCM results show that Brady restructurers had more favorable outcomes compared to synthetic controls on public debt, external debt, real GDP growth, and inflation. Brady restructurers also saw an increase in trade openness and their FDI stock relative to the synthetic control. They also experienced a faster and larger turnaround in their current account balances around 1993.

Accounting for variation in the timing of Brady restructurings confirms the main findings of this Element. These results from a staggered DiD are summarized in Figures 34–41, which are consistent with the original DiD presented previously. The staggered treatment, which studies the impact of Brady restructurings before and after the start of the Brady restructuring, showed some

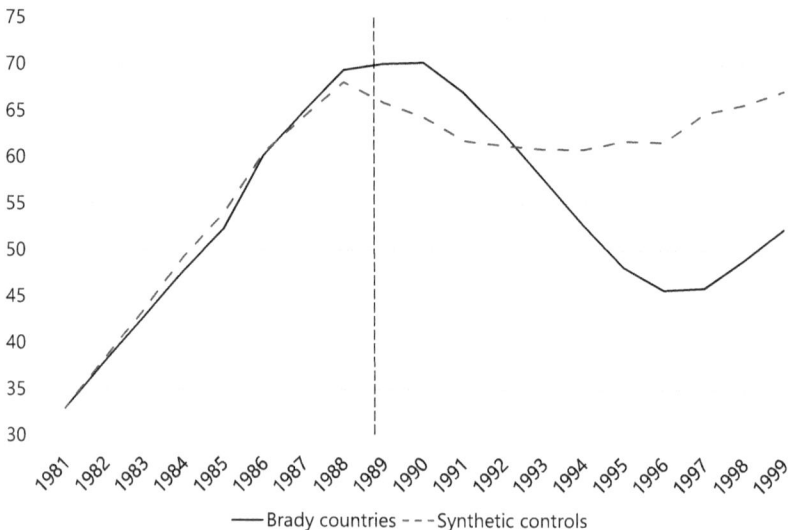

Figure 27 Public debt, % of GDP (SCM)

Source: Table 2 and authors' calculations

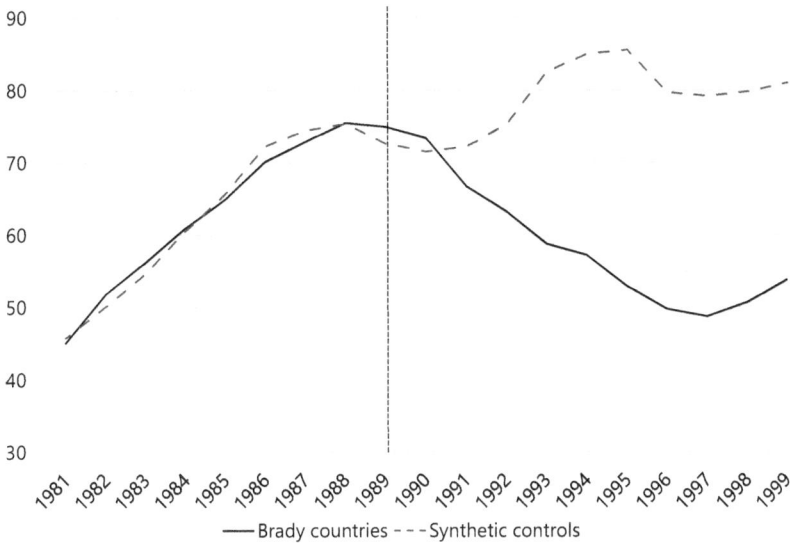

Figure 28 External debt, % of GDP (SCM)

Source: Table 2 and authors' calculations

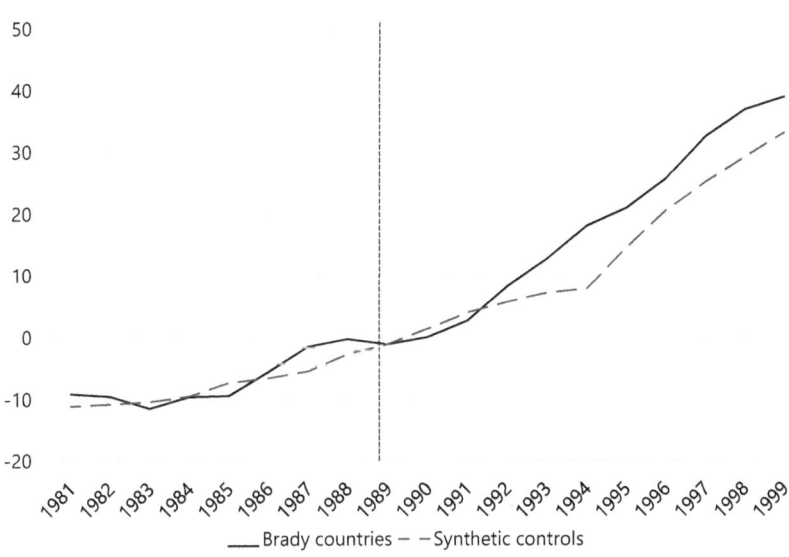

Figure 29 Real GDP, % deviation from 1989 (SCM)

Source: Table 2 and authors' calculations

improvement in the years running up to the Brady exchanges. This improvement could reflect confidence effects provided by the announcement of the Brady Plan, of which Arslanalp and Henry (2005) provide evidence. Another

Figure 30 Trade openness, % of GDP (SCM)

Source: Table 2 and authors' calculations

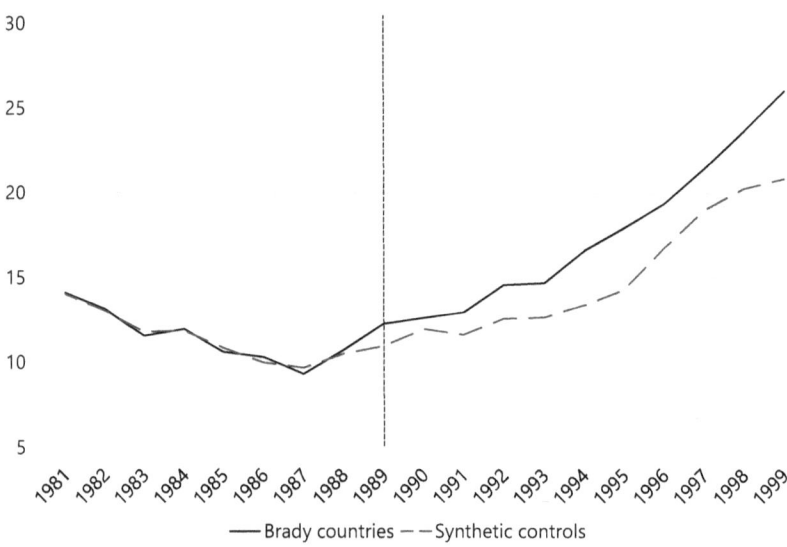

Figure 31 FDI stock, share of external liabilities (SCM)

Source: Table 2 and authors' calculations

potential explanation is that the prior actions taken by Brady restructurers, including through the Baker Plan and other policy actions required to achieve UCT quality IMF programs, yielded early dividends prior to the agreement of debt relief under the Brady Plan.

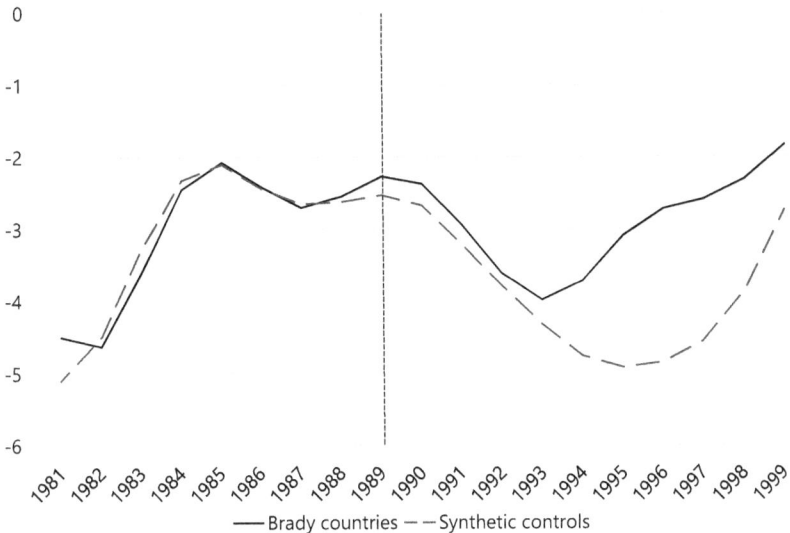

Figure 32 Current account, % of GDP (SCM)

Source: Table 2 and authors' calculations

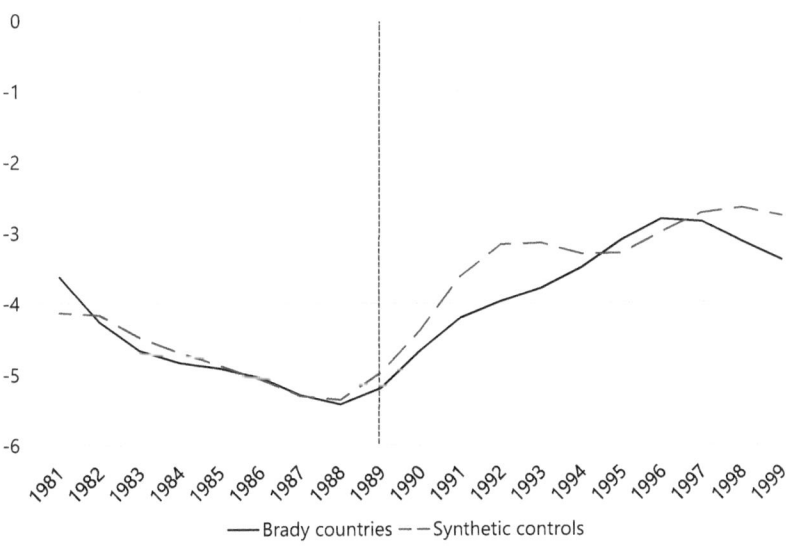

Figure 33 Net investment income, % of GDP

Source: Table 2 and authors' calculations (SCM)

4.4 Summary

This section provided an empirical analysis of the macroeconomic impact of the Brady Plan. It compared the outcomes of Brady countries with a control group of fifty EMDEs that did not receive debt relief under the Brady Plan. The

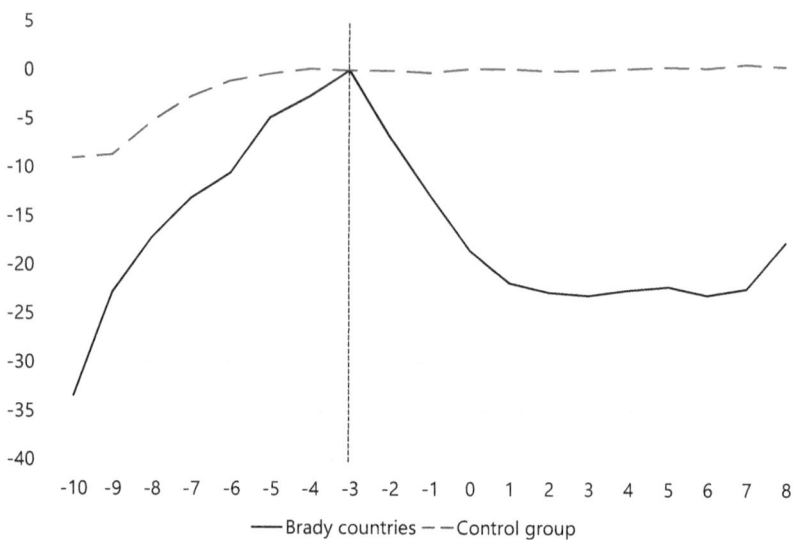

Figure 34 Public debt, % of GDP (staggered DiD)

Source: Table 2 and authors' calculations

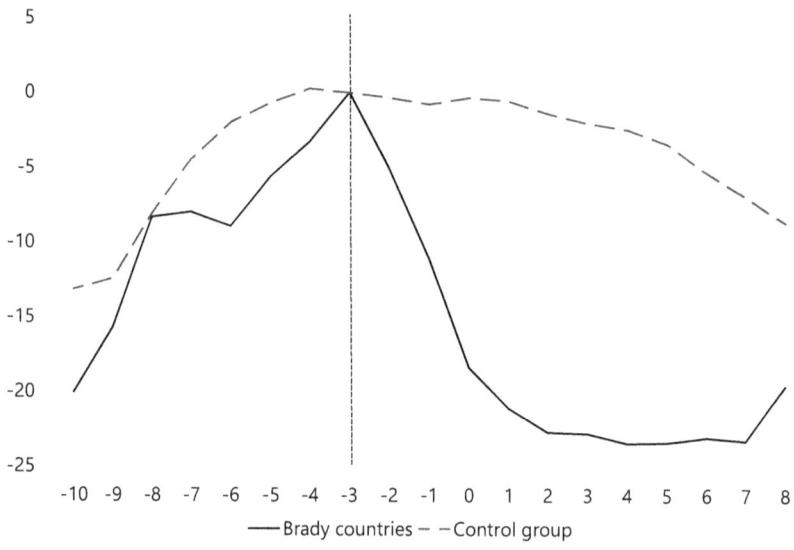

Figure 35 External debt, % of GDP (staggered DiD)

Source: Table 2 and authors' calculations

empirical strategy used DiD and SCM to address the nonrandom nature of achieving debt relief treatment. The analysis includes ten Brady countries: Argentina, Brazil, Costa Rica, Dominican Republic, Ecuador, Jordan,

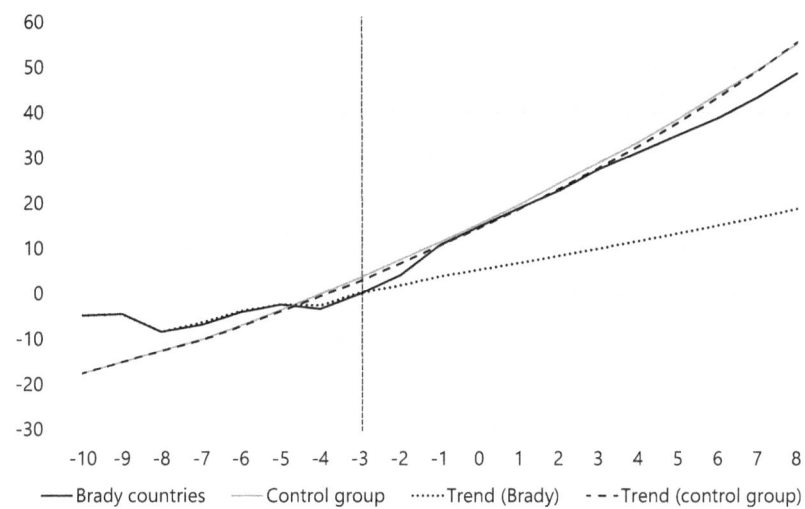

Figure 36 Real GDP, relative to trend three years before Brady deal
Source: Table 2 and authors' calculations (staggered DiD)

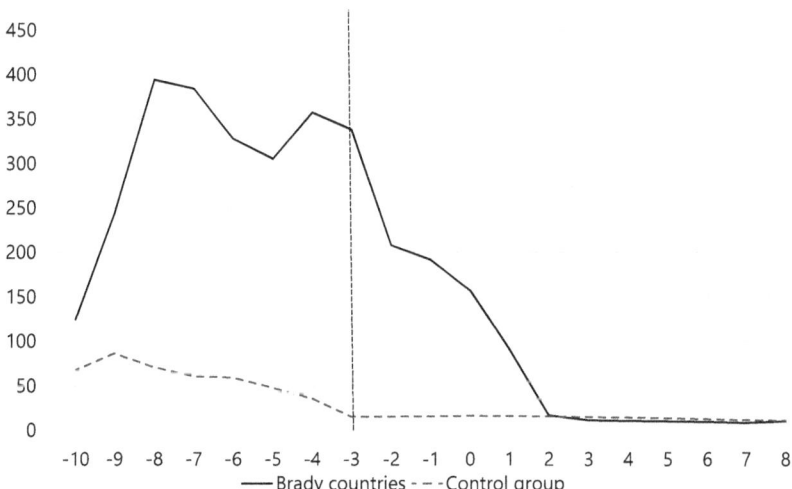

Figure 37 Inflation, three-year average of GDP deflator growth, %
(staggered DiD)

Source: Table 2 and authors' calculations

Mexico, Nigeria, Peru, and the Philippines. The control group consists of seventeen countries that received debt restructuring between 1970 and 2013 but did not sign Brady deals, and twenty-three other EMDEs that did not seek debt treatments. The DiD regression assessed the impact of Brady restructurings

Figure 38 Trade openness, % of GDP (staggered DiD)

Source: Table 2 and authors' calculations

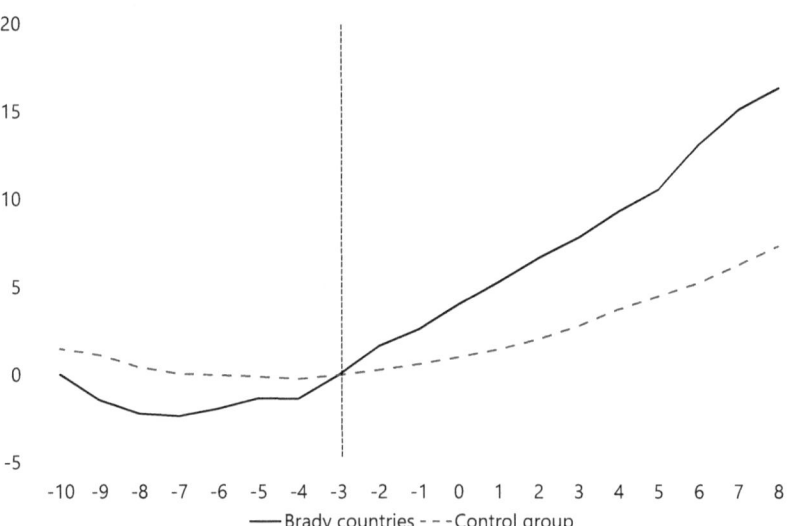

Figure 39 FDI stock, share of external liabilities (staggered DiD)

Source: Table 2 and authors' calculations

on various macroeconomic variables. Additionally, the SCM estimated a counterfactual for the outcome variables using a weighted average of observations from the control group. This approach helped isolate the effect of the Brady Plan from other factors.

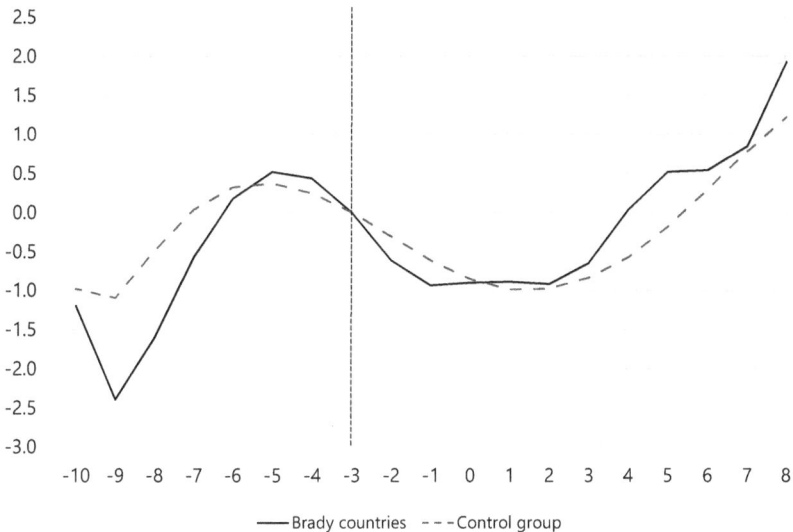

Figure 40 Current account, % of GDP (staggered DiD)

Source: Table 2 and authors' calculations

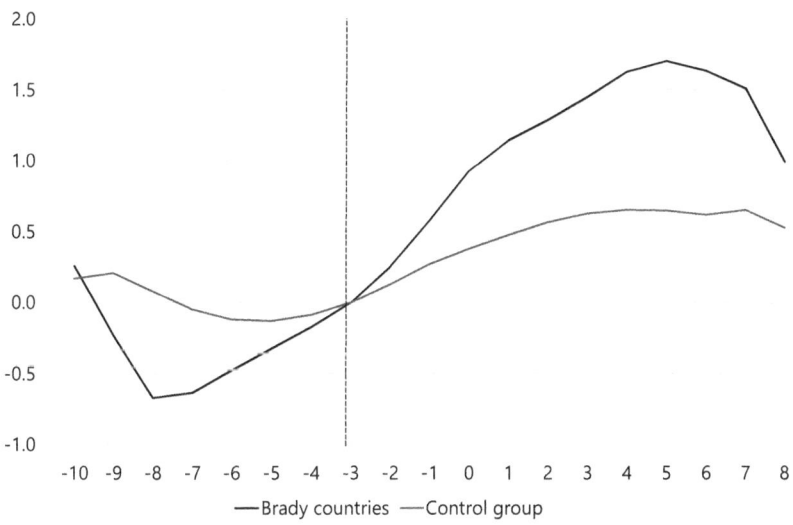

Figure 41 Net investment income, % of GDP (staggered DiD)

Source: Table 2 and authors' calculations

The analysis showed that public debt levels of Brady countries dropped by 20 percentage points of GDP relative to non-Brady countries in the decade following the first Brady deal. External debt burdens also fell by roughly 25 percentage points relative to the control group. Real GDP growth in Brady countries more than doubled to 3.4 percent per year in the decade following the first Brady deal, compared to 1.5 percent per year before the restructurings. Inflation rates in Brady countries declined significantly relative to the control group. Brady countries achieved faster growth through greater integration into global trade and direct investment. Trade openness increased, and the share of FDI in external liabilities rose significantly. Net resource inflows into Brady countries increased, providing space for growth-enhancing imports. Higher TFP growth was the main driver of the economic growth following Brady restructurings.

The baseline DiD results are consistent with the SCM findings. Brady restructurers had more favorable outcomes compared to synthetic controls on public debt, external debt, real GDP growth, and inflation. The staggered DiD approach confirms the main findings, showing improvement in the years leading up to the Brady exchanges. The Brady Plan had a significant positive impact on the macroeconomic performance of Brady countries, leading to lower debt levels, higher economic growth, and improved integration into global trade and investment. The structural reforms undertaken by Brady countries – which outperformed peers as measured by performance on IMF programs and different measures of product and financial market openness – likely contributed to these outcomes, highlighting the effectiveness of the Brady Plan in addressing debt sustainability challenges via both debt relief and providing a framework for structural reforms. A summary of the average treatment effects using the three methods is presented in Table 8. The results are broadly consistent.

It should be acknowledged that there are methodological challenges in empirical macroeconomics that should be considered when evaluating the

Table 8 Comparison of treatment effects (indicative)

	DiD	SCM	SDiD	Average
Public debt	−18.4	−19.0	−18.1	−18.5
External debt	−19.4	−29.6	−10.9	−20.0
Real GDP	24.4	5.8	30.3	20.2
Trade openness	11.9	12.9	11.3	12.0
FDI stock	8.4	3.9	9.0	7.1

Note: The table summarizes the average treatment effects of Brady countries for several variables using the Element's various empirical methods. DID and SCM results include the cumulative impact from 1989 to 1999. The SDID shows the 10-year impact following the date of treatment. Public debt and external debt are in percentage of GDP. Real GDP is in cumulative percentage change from 1989 trend. Trade openness and FDI stock are in percentage points of GDP.

arguments made in this Element. This Element presents evidence that Brady restructurers achieved better macroeconomic outcomes than non-Brady peers. However, it can only speculate on the potential causal links between Brady exchanges and better macroeconomic outcomes – there is no definitive empirical method to assess granular causal mechanisms between debt relief and better outcomes. Additionally, this Element is limited by a lack of data availability in parts, with reliable data available for ten out of sixteen total Brady restructurers. The limited sample size of data available may bias the Element's empirical results, though the authors do not have strong reason to believe the omitted countries would have drastically changed the Element's bottom-line conclusions. Moreover, assessing the applicability of the Brady Plan today is difficult given differences in global macroeconomic conditions and the international financial landscape between the Brady period and today.

Having explained how the original Brady Plan delivered on debt relief using multiple empirical methods, this Element now turns to the policy implications that follow from this analysis, taking stock of the current debt architecture and analyzing how Brady mechanisms could complement the existing architecture while considering key differences in the Brady period and today.

5 Policy Implications

Having discussed how the Brady Plan contributed to improved macroeconomic outcomes for Brady restructurers, this Element examines the current state of the international architecture for debt restructuring. It surveys the features and limitations of the current debt architecture, highlighting the incentives that tend to bias the system toward providing "too little, too late" debt relief for distressed sovereigns. It then summarizes some policy implications of the Brady Plan for today while detailing additional operational aspects that should be considered before a twenty-first century Brady Plan is undertaken.

5.1 Current Features and Recent Developments in the Global Debt Architecture

In the wake of the COVID-19 crisis, debt relief featured prominently in multilateral and bilateral support packages to countries hit by the pandemic. Most actions focused on near-term liquidity support rather than systemic efforts to provide face value haircuts to sovereigns at or near debt distress (i.e., solvency support). In May 2020, the G20 launched the DSSI for all countries eligible for International Development Association (IDA) loans. The DSSI allowed for a rescheduling of bilateral principal and interest payments coming due to official creditors for three years with a one-year grace period. These reschedulings were meant to be NPV neutral, with no face value reductions. Despite the lack of significant NPV reductions, the DSSI provided meaningful liquidity relief for forty-eight IDA-eligible countries, with about $13 billion in suspended debt-service payments from May 2020 through December 2021 (World Bank, 2022a).[54] Several IFIs participated in providing debt service suspension (i.e., flow relief), such as through the IMF's Catastrophe Containment and Relief Trust (IMF).

Subsequently, the G20 and Paris Club created the Common Framework (CF) for Debt Treatments beyond the DSSI to promote creditor coordination for debt restructuring. All DSSI-eligible countries were able to request a CF debt treatment, and as of end-2024, four countries requested debt treatments through the CF: Chad, Ethiopia, Ghana, and Zambia. Since the pandemic, there have also been several ad hoc debt restructurings for vulnerable middle-income countries, such as for Sri Lanka and Suriname. These efforts took place at the same time as major liquidity operations undertaken by AE central banks and other financial institutions, though much of this support has been withdrawn as of end-2024 (see Figure 4).[55]

One of the challenges today is that some major creditors are not members of the Paris Club. Thus, considerable diplomatic effort has been expended by multilaterals and leading countries to bring these creditors into existing institutions, such as via the CF. Progress on CF cases has improved as the major players gained experience and common understanding was achieved. For instance, timelines from IMF Staff-Level Agreements (SLA) to delivering financing assurances from official creditors required for IMF programs declined

---

[54] DSSI was a milestone in sovereign debt restructuring because it was the first time since China's emergence as a key bilateral creditor that many non-Paris Club creditors such as China participated in a debt relief initiative. According to one study by Bräutigam and Huang, Chinese creditors contributed nearly two-thirds of notional debt service suspensions during the DSSI period. This effort is commensurate to China's credit exposure to many low-income countries, with Chinese creditors accounting for nearly 30 percent of all claims for DSSI-eligible countries. See (Bräutigam & Huang, 2023).

[55] For example, since the pandemic, reserve currency issuing central banks significantly increased their balance sheets and cut their policy rates. They engaged in different types of liquidity operations, with positive systemic spillovers. For instance, the United States Federal Reserve launched several US dollar swap lines with other central banks to ease dollar funding strains. The Federal Reserve also introduced the Foreign and International Monetary Authorities (FIMA) repo facility, in which foreign central banks can get access to US dollars by pledging high-quality dollar securities (e.g., US Treasury securities) as collateral. Other sources of unconditional liquidity included the IMF's $650 billion allocation of Special Drawing Rights (SDRs) in August 2021, emergency and UCT-quality IMF programs, and other forms of multilateral and bilateral support for credit constrained and other debt vulnerable countries. Subsequently, the rise in inflation globally led to a withdrawal of support and tightening of financial conditions, which could exacerbate pre-existing debt vulnerabilities by raising interest expenses on variable and maturing loans, potentially crowding out other essential spending at a time of rising geoeconomic fragmentation and trade policy uncertainty (International Monetary Fund, 2023b).

significantly since the CF was launched, with Ghana taking about five months from SLA to IMF program approval – roughly half the time it took Chad and Zambia.[56] Progress on debt restructuring has also been enhanced by the IMF, World Bank, and G20 GSDR, which helped foster a common understanding on technical issues in debt restructuring, including comparability of treatment, restructuring perimeters, information sharing underlying IMF and World Bank staff debt sustainability analyses, and various restructuring processes. The result of these efforts is greater mutual understanding among the major sovereign debt players and thus a more effective architecture despite the more variegated creditor landscape (Pazarbasioglu, 2024).[57] These developments also show the capacity of the international financial architecture to evolve and undertake policy innovation to achieve cooperative outcomes.

These efforts have not been a panacea but have nonetheless helped with restructuring processes. In one of the CF cases in which creditors agreed to a debt treatment, Chad – which was indebted to a large commodity trading company Glencore – its restructured debt did not contain significant face value haircuts.[58] Rather, the agreement included a reprofiling of payments coming due with a promise for creditors to reconvene should the price of oil – Chad's primary export – fall and thus create renewed debt sustainability challenges (Bretton Woods Project, 2022). In Zambia's case, which agreed to a CF treatment with its creditor committee on June 22, 2023, the restructuring was viewed as a positive step and possibly a template for future restructurings (George, 2023; Georgieva, 2023; Yellen, 2023b).[59] For Ethiopia, the use of recent IMF reforms to the debt restructuring process, including deeming CF proceedings as so-called credible official creditor processes, helped provide financing assurances for their IMF program and unlock new financing for the country (International Monetary Fund, 2025b).[60] This progress follows from strong multilateral efforts and a positive response to overcome initial reluctance of some bilateral official creditors to form creditor committees and furnish timely data on their sovereign claims at

---

[56] For a recent analysis of Ghana's CF treatment, see (Grogorian & Vessereau, 2024).
[57] Drawing data from over 170 interviews, Huang and Bräutigam link China's increasing cooperation with multilateral debt restructuring frameworks to their bureaucrats' socialization into the multilateral regime. Their article thus supports the view that mutual understanding achieved via multilateralism can lead to more cooperative outcomes in global economic governance, see (Huang & Bräutigam, 2025).
[58] See, inter alia (Georgieva & Pazarbasioglu, 2021) and (Ahmed & Brown, 2022).
[59] Former US Treasury Secretary Janet Yellen recently noted that the publication of a user guide for distressed borrowers may enhance future CF treatments, see (Yellen, 2023c).
[60] For more on the IMF's recent debt policy reforms, see (International Monetary Fund, 2024a). For additional background on the IMF's financing assurances policy and role in debt restructuring, see (International Monetary Fund, 2024b). For a good summary of the IMF's views on the sovereign debt restructuring architecture, including some limitations, see IMF (2020a).

times, which delayed restructuring processes. Potential causes of this lack of initial creditor coordination among new official bilateral creditors could have been due to their limited experience in multilateral debt restructuring efforts, a lack of internal coordination at the domestic level to report on sovereign exposures and slow domestic approval processes to provide relief, or an unwillingness to participate in sovereign debt restructuring and offer comparability of treatment, among other potential claims (Setser, 2023a; Wigglesworth & Yu, 2023; Makoff, Maret, & Wright, 2025).[61]

More broadly, limited participation may reflect fundamental incentives on the part of both debtors and creditors to "play for time" when faced with potential debt distress. Several studies have examined the strategic interaction between creditors and debtors in the context of debt negotiations and find that multiple stakeholders in the debt restructuring process have an incentive to "extend and pretend" by rescheduling debts coming due but not changing the face value of existing obligations.[62] As an example, given uncertainty about debt dynamics, IFIs may not be willing to conclude that debts are unsustainable and must thus be restructured, particularly when their own lending cannot proceed without an assessment of debt sustainability. Also, many IFIs can have a bias toward optimistic forecasts (Loungani et al., 2023).[63] Critically, bilateral official creditors would rather avoid frontloaded losses and give indebted creditors time to achieve sustainability exclusively through adjustment, rather than making concessions preemptively, so the official sector also has an incentive to play for time. PSI has also been limited in some restructuring cases, despite the development of a Terms of Reference for comparable treatment prepared by the Institute for International Finance (Talero, 2022), potentially reflecting similar dynamics. And debtors themselves may also be reluctant to ask their creditors for debt relief, given the potential reputational risk of early restructurings, including such requests being viewed as unfavorable by the CRAs.[64] Debtors may also fear future market access and/or higher borrowing costs post-restructuring (Cruces & Trebesch, 2013). These strategic interactions among IFIs, the official sector, and the private sector are seen to drive delays in restructuring. Sean Hagan and Brad Setser also argue

---

[61] For a critical view of the "toxic geopolitics" potentially impacting the CF and related multilateral efforts, see (Bräutigam, 2023).

[62] See, for example, (Pitchford & Wright, 2010) and (Benjamin & Wright, 2019). For an alternative view of IMF forecasts in the context of debt restructurings from the private sector perspective, including the contention that IMF staff forecasts are too pessimistic in some recent restructuring contexts, see (Virketis, 2024).

[63] See also (Baqir, Ramcharan, & Sahay, 2005) on optimism in IMF growth and inflation forecasts in IMF programs. Beaudry and Willems (2022) find that overly optimistic growth forecasts induce economic contractions a few years later by accumulating excessive public and private debt, see (Beaudry & Willems, 2022).

[64] See (United Nations, 2022) and (Fitch Ratings, 2021).

that the de facto sequential nature of debt restructuring contributes to these delays. Thus, to speed up restructurings, they suggest the development of a "Coordinated Framework" to allow for simultaneous decision-making across creditor classes, both official and private (Hagan & Setser, 2024), rather than deciding PSI after an official treatment, which could lead to another round of negotiations requested by the official sector.[65]

The tendency to extend and pretend has costs. Protracted debt restructurings are often accompanied by a lack of new external financing, which could make macroeconomic stabilization trade-offs more acute while potentially inducing pro-cyclical policies (e.g., tightening the fiscal stance during a period of soft growth). Asonuma et al. further find that longer restructuring periods are associated with larger output costs compared to faster restructurings. Critically, preemptive restructurings – or restructuring prior to default – mitigate output and banking sector costs that tend to be associated with debt restructurings (Asonuma et al., 2019).[66]

The sovereign debt architecture also faces pre-COVID challenges, which can impact the timeliness of debt restructuring. Some of these limitations include the lack of collective voting features in syndicated loans; a lack of widespread use of SCDIs in market-based mechanisms as well, possibly due to their cost or absence of investor appetite; issues in debt transparency, including the use of nondisclosure agreements in official bilateral lending; and the existence of opaque collateralized debt contracts (with unrelated collateral), among others. Together, these factors can combine to produce a debt restructuring landscape in which multiple players are incentivized to bargain for time to attain a better payout; individual bilateral official creditors may wield outsize influence; credit events can sometimes lead to a loss of ownership and therefore sovereignty for the debtor; and the development of a debt profile that lacks robustness to exogenous shocks.[67] Any potential reforms to the sovereign debt architecture should thus seek to remedy these issues, including changing the incentives of

---

[65] The Zambia debt restructuring involved such a sequence, wherein an official sector creditor believed that PSI was not comparable to the official treatment, thus reopening another round of negotiations with bondholders. See (Makoff, Maret, & Wright, 2025).

[66] Hence, efforts to strengthen the global debt architecture should continue, including via the GSDR and other multilateral efforts, such as the IMF–World Bank three-pillar approach, to improve creditor coordination, safeguard economic reform momentum, reducing stigma associated with requesting IMF programs and debt treatments, among others, all of which can help disincentivize "extend and pretend" dynamics while reducing the stigma of countries facing debt distress coming early for debt treatments. On the three-pillar approach, see (International Monetary Fund and World Bank, 2024).

[67] See (Sobel, 2022) for an overview of existing institutional challenges in the sovereign debt architecture, as well as (Sobel, 2016) on the specific challenges related to operationalizing an SDRM, including skepticism for such a mechanism from the US Treasury, and on the development of an international consensus on CACs as an alternative to a SDRM. For another

both creditors and debtors to play for time; achieving higher rates of participation from both the official and the private sector; attaining realistic assumptions about the need for and appropriate balance between debt relief and adjustment; and having a credible strategy for dealing with potential spoilers, including holdouts.[68]

5.2 Historic Benefits of the Brady Plan, Lessons for Today, and Operational Considerations

Based on the results of this study, the Brady Plan can rightly be viewed as a success as judged from the standpoint of enhancing the macroeconomic performance of Brady restructurers, safeguarding their capacity to repay their restructured debt, strengthening their market access, and improving the liquidity of their restructured claims. So, there is prima facie evidence that Brady-style restructuring mechanisms can be useful tools in a diverse toolkit of debt relief. Still, simply rebooting the Brady Plan would not solve all of the existing challenges in the sovereign debt landscape. Such a reboot would need to consider novel challenges and address issues associated with domestic debt, creditor coordination and the emergence of new creditor classes (with commensurately more complicated seniority structures of existing claims), and systemic incentives for creditors and debtors to play for time. This section summarizes some of the historic benefits of the Brady Plan that follow from the study's empirical analysis while attempting to draw some lessons for the present period given differences in the architecture from the late 1980s.

Brady exchanges achieved faster and more durable debt stock reduction, with macroeconomic dividends for debtors. As shown in Section 3, Brady exchanges led to significant and persistent declines in public and external debt for Brady restructurers relative to the control group. Additionally, Brady restructurers saw better macroeconomic outcomes, including faster growth, relative to the non-Brady control group. Taken together, the "multiplier" effect of the face value reductions on debt burdens of the Brady countries was particularly large, indicating that Brady-style mechanisms were effective tools for debt relief. This result is consistent with recent research on debt reductions, as discussed in International Monetary Fund (2023a).

---

perspective, see (Guzman, Ocampo, & Stiglitz, 2016). For a detailed account of Argentina's 2001 default and subsequent negotiations, including in the context of a potential SDRM and eventual move toward CACs to address the holdout creditor issue, see (Makoff, 2024).

[68] See (Fang, Schumacher, & Trebesch, 2021) and (Alfaro, 2015) on the impact of holdouts on the sovereign debt restructuring process. For a recent analysis of the international financial architecture for sovereign debt resolution, see (Farah-Yacoub, Graf von Luckner, & Grund, 2025).

The Brady Plan had the benefit of converting illiquid and nontransparent claims into marketable securities, which offered liquidity benefits for creditors and debtors. Commercial banks – many of which originally intended to hold their sovereign loans to maturity – were given the opportunity to turn illiquid loans into tradeable securities, thereby strengthening the liquidity of restructured claims while reducing creditor concentration (Miles, 1999).[69] Brady bonds opened new categories of institutional investors that were attracted to the relatively higher returns offered by Brady bonds while still seeking the safety provided by their collateralized structure. This potential benefit is further evidenced by the fact that external sovereign bonds generally offer returns in excess of the compensation for the risk of default, while the same may not necessarily be true for bilateral claims (Meyer, Reinhart, & Trebesch, 2022). Today, many low-income country debts are being held to maturity by bilateral sovereign creditors for which there is little trading of existing claims. Should these bilateral creditors want to turn their illiquid claims into tradeable securities while, over time, potentially decreasing their exposure, then Brady-style mechanisms could again be useful, particularly if face value write-downs are needed to restore sustainability for debtors.

Brady-style restructurings allow creditors and debtors alike to reissue debt with the newest features available, some of which may not have been available at the time original debts were contracted. For instance, tranched structures with different return profiles based on assumed risk of loss could be used. Additional option-like features could be embedded in restructured claims, such as SCDIs, which link interest payments to other conditions, such as GDP, commodity prices, or discrete events. Similarly, VRIs could also be included, as they were during the Brady era or more recently implemented in the restructuring of Suriname, which had a VRI linked to oil prices in its restructured debt, see (Campos, Do Rosario, & Kuipers, 2023).[70] An additional option would be to include debt-for-nature swap-like features, which include debt relief in exchange for commitments to use added fiscal space for climate mitigation and adaptation. At the same time, the uptake of these structures has been limited and would ultimately depend on debtors' interest and ability to offer these features. Still, Brady exchanges afford the opportunity to explore and deploy these mechanisms in restructured debt, which can be useful in some cases.

Historically, Brady exchanges helped reduce the incentive for creditors to hold out in debt restructuring. As mentioned in Section 2, there are incentives

---

[69] Of course, creditors may need to overcome domestic legal constraints that would hamper their willingness to convert existing bilateral loans into tradeable bonds, such as obtaining parliamentary approval.

[70] See also (International Monetary Fund, 2023c).

for bilateral and commercial creditors to refuse to agree to a debt restructuring and hold out, including a desire to give troubled sovereigns more time to improve sustainability via adjustment, a lack of internal coordination within creditor governments to achieve consensus on a restructuring, and an incentive to free ride on other creditors' forbearance, among others. Today, the collateralized structure of Brady exchanges could incentivize potential holdouts to agree to a restructuring by reducing potential future losses and providing confidence that restructured debts will continue to be serviced. Thus, Brady exchanges can reduce the risk to creditors of serial defaults.

Policy commitments achieved through Brady-style restructurings – including through IMF programs – helped foster macroeconomic sustainability and safeguard reform momentum among debtors. The empirical results of this Element show that Brady restructurers had more favorable outcomes relative to the control group, driven mainly by the sharp pickup in productivity growth of Brady countries in the 1990s. IMF programs and other macroeconomic stabilization programs can serve as commitment devices of Brady restructurers to undertake needed but potentially difficult-to-implement reforms, as was the case in the original Brady Plan. Brady relief can also serve as a commitment device for restructurers to agree to programs while avoiding potentially rosy scenarios in restructurers' macroeconomic frameworks.

A puzzle is why Brady-style mechanisms were so successful in achieving better macroeconomic outcomes, whereas some other debt relief episodes offer mixed results on debt relief. One potential explanation for this favorable result is that the Brady Plan coupled debt relief with strong macroeconomic adjustment, along with structural reforms, as well as the fact that Brady restructurers were relatively more developed as compared to, for example, HIPC restructurers. It is also possible that the years of MYRAs and Baker-era support helped pave the way for the productivity gains observed once creditors delivered debt relief.

During the Brady period and today, addressing unsustainable debt burdens could have had positive systemic spillovers. Today, given the beneficial impact of Brady-style restructurings on fiscal space, it is possible that Brady restructurers can relax the fiscal-related constraints on growth. This newfound fiscal space, if used wisely, can be deployed for priority investments, including resilience-building and adaptation to shared challenges (e.g., climate finance), with positive externalities to the rest of the global economy.[71] Additionally, given existing macroeconomic linkages and improved macroeconomic

---

[71] Indeed, several Brady deals included provisions to allocate some of the space provided by debt relief to environmental projects; see (Sarkar, 1994).

performance, Brady restructurings can have growth, trade, and investment spillovers for trading partners, which can improve global macroeconomic stability and dynamism.

Despite its historic benefits, Brady-style restructurings would not be a panacea to solve debt sustainability and debt restructuring challenges today. The results of this study show that the Brady Plan's success applied to debtors under specific conditions relating to, inter-alia, countries that previously had market access and had been targets for the original Baker Plan due to commercial banks' outsize exposure to them; creditors' desire to achieve assurances about debtors' capacity-to-repay via policy adjustment and collateralization; existing claims that would benefit from enhanced liquidity and securitization; debtors willing to undertake ambitious reforms anchored by strong performance under IMF programs to achieve debt relief; and creditors willing to provide substantial face value relief. Critically, most Brady restructurers also had a modicum of institutional strength.[72] The global macroeconomic conjuncture today is also different from the Brady period: The original Brady deals also took place during a time of strong global economic growth and a relatively favorable commodity price outlook, which can be contrasted to the tepid growth and uncertain commodity price outlook today. Moreover, many vulnerable countries today are LICs with external debt held by official sector creditors. More work would need to be done to assess the potential benefits of collateralized restructured instruments for these types of debtors, including those that lacked market access prior to experiencing debt challenges.

The current period bears similarities and differences to the 1980s that should be considered in any systemic debt restructuring plan using Brady-style mechanisms. As was the case in the 1980s, any systemic debt treatment plan to assist troubled sovereigns should consider the implications of write-downs on creditor capitalization, the more variegated creditor landscape today, additional similarities and differences in the global macroeconomic conjuncture, and the diversity of crisis-fighting strategies among debtors today compared to the original Brady period. A summary of these considerations is presented in Table 9.

Before considering debt relief initiatives, including those offered by Brady-style restructuring mechanisms, the exposure of creditors to distressed and highly indebted sovereigns would need to be assessed. In the 1980s, commercial banks faced material recapitalization risks associated with debt distress among heavily indebted countries. This was one of the reasons banks were initially reluctant to agree to face value write-downs. These risks had been substantially reduced by 1989 due to, in part, early liquidity support to distressed sovereigns via IMF programs and the Baker Plan. In fact, it is possible the sequencing of the

---

[72] See Arslanalp and Henry (2006).

Table 9 Comparing the sovereign debt landscape of the 1980s and 2020s

	1980s	2020s
Global macro conditions	Tightening financing conditions due to rising inflation; declining commodities terms of trade; decade of restructuring (1990s) broadly viewed as a period of relative prosperity in the global economy	Tightening financial conditions due to rising inflation; increasing commodities terms of trade with an uncertain trajectory; decade of restructurings (2020s) projected to have a weak outlook
Target countries	Heavily indebted EMs	EMs and LICs
Liquidity transformation	Turned illiquid into liquid claims	Could turn illiquid (i.e., bilateral official or private) into liquid claims, or restructure existing liquid claims (e.g., Eurobonds) while introducing new features
Creditor base	Concentrated among commercial banks and Paris Club creditors	Diffused among commercial creditors, non-Paris Club bilateral creditors (many LICs), and market-based creditors (e.g., Eurobonds among many EMs)
Creditor solvency challenges/ exposure to distressed sovereigns	Binding constraint, with concerns about impairments among incumbent creditors (primarily commercial)	Potentially less binding, with fewer concerns about impairments among incumbent creditors (in some cases, primarily bilateral)

Table 9 (cont.)

	1980s	2020s
Crisis management strategies	Narrow, anchored by IMF programs	Broader, facilitated by a more diverse global financial safety net
Global consensus	Strong global consensus and declining geopolitical competition	Rising fragmentation and more prominent geopolitical competition
Sponsorship	United States and G7	Potential sponsors include the United States, group of non-US G7 countries, non-Paris Club creditors, or an IFI
Case-by-case or systematic?	Case-by-case	Likely continued case-by-case

Source: Truman (2020), Sobel (2022), Aiyar, Ilyina, & Others (2023), and authors.

Baker-Brady periods may have contributed to the favorable macroeconomic outcomes of Brady restructurers. Specifically, debt write-downs may not be feasible given existing political economy constraints until incumbent creditors rebuild their capital bases. Hence, the Brady Plan showed that the timing of stages of debt relief needs to balance reforms, providing assistance via debt relief and new financing, and avoiding undue cost to exposed creditors. Today, bank exposure to this market segment has declined. Some sovereign lenders could have the balance sheet strength needed to absorb losses without triggering widespread financial distress.[73] Still, more work would need to be done to

---

[73] Makoff and coworkers analyze the financial capacity of China Eximbank to absorb losses. They argue that based on China Eximbank's 2022 financial statements, China has a return on assets of about 0.14 percent. The authors conclude that this level of return on assets implies that China Eximbank has little loss absorption capacity. To address domestic coordination challenges and consolidate China's overseas claims, the authors argue that China should establish a sovereign debt asset management company, akin to the good bank–bad bank structures created in China during the 1990s to address its commercial banking crisis (Makoff, Maret, & Wright, 2025, pp. 28–33). Notwithstanding the novelty of such a good bank–bad bank approach, to the extent that China Eximbank has both explicit and implicit support from China's government, and given the policy space available to China, it follows that China Eximbank could have greater loss absorption capacity than what would be implied by a narrow reading on its reported net profit and return on assets. In either case, more work would need to be done to analyze these exposures and ensure that debt write-downs do not cause undue economic harm to incumbent creditors, which could jeopardize the future flow of financing.

assess the capacity of incumbent creditors to absorb losses while putting into place mitigation measures should these institutions prove systemically important. Such analysis would also need to consider how write-downs could impact the future availability of flow of financing to distressed sovereigns as well.

Differences in creditor base composition could make creditor coordination more challenging today. As explained previously, the sovereign creditor base was relatively more concentrated in the 1980s, with commercial banks and bilateral Paris Club creditors primarily exposed to heavily indebted countries. Today, the creditor landscape is considerably more diverse, with a larger role for private creditors, market-based financing, and the emergence of bilateral non-Paris Club lenders.[74] As a result, the Paris Club is less representative today than it was in the 1980s (World Bank, 2022c).

Macroeconomic conditions are similar, but the outlook in the 2020s may be worse than that of the 1990s. Both the 1980s and 2020s had periods characterized by rising inflation and tighter AE monetary policy, a stronger dollar and higher borrowing costs among EMs and LICs. Similarly, both periods have seen a global growth slowdown. All of these factors contribute to rising debt vulnerabilities. One of the potential reasons for the original Brady Plan's success was the strong global growth of the 1990s that followed the first Brady restructuring. In comparison, the current growth outlook appears tepid, and thus any debt restructuring effort may not be able to count on a favorable macroeconomic conjuncture going forward. Given rising geoeconomic fragmentation, countries may not be able to count on favorable foreign demand and other benefits offered by the liberal global trading system to boost growth, instead relying on domestic drivers of growth. In other words, fragmentation presents novel challenges to countries' growth models, with the tailwinds of globalization shifting potentially to headwinds of global protectionism and further fragmentation (Aiyar, Ilyina, & Others, 2023).[75] Additionally, the global interest rate outlook today and during the Brady period are different, which could impact the efficacy of using zero-coupon bonds as collateral for Brady bonds, as well as funding of these purchases using variable rates funded by IFIs.[76] Another key difference between the original Brady period and today is the commodity price outlook: The 1990s was generally a period of subdued commodity prices and favorable commodities terms of trade for net importers, while in the early 2020s, the commodity terms of trade are increasing. In the

---

[74] See (Dielmann, 2021) for a summary of the rise in cross-border lending by non-Paris Club creditors, as well as an assessment of the terms and implications of such lending.

[75] For an additional study of the impact on geoeconomic fragmentation on trade and output losses, including on LICs, see (Bolhuis, Chen, & Kett, 2023). See also (Gopinath, 2023).

[76] For more on these potential differences, see (Setser, 2024).

longer term, the commodity price outlook is uncertain given the importance of the green transition for demand and supply of individual commodities and broader trade fragmentation (International Monetary Fund, 2023d).

In terms of tools available to distressed sovereigns, crisis fighting strategies are more diverse today than they were in the Brady period. At the time of the original Brady Plan, the IFIs, commercial banks, and bilateral creditors were the primary creditors for distressed sovereigns. Additional layers in the global financial safety net, such as regional financing arrangements, were less relevant in the 1980s. Today, distressed sovereigns have access to diverse sources of financing, including precautionary tools including central bank swap lines and central bank repo facilities (e.g., FIMA) (Truman, 2020). There is also evidence that non-Paris Club lenders are willing to provide crisis financing to countries in distress.[77] Sovereigns may therefore have a higher bar to requesting debt treatments as they may first seek to exhaust all other options available, including liquidity support instruments. The availability of other financing sources could also complicate the coordination challenges facing distressed sovereigns and their creditors – for example by multiplying the number of players for whom comparability of treatment should be assessed – as more parties may have a stake in the outcome of a debt restructuring.

Any plan for systemic debt relief would require a willing party – likely a sovereign, group of sovereigns, or IFI – to underwrite the plan. In the 1980s, the United States in close collaboration with Japan underwrote the Brady Plan by providing enhancements for interest and principal payments on the restructured bonds. For instance, the US Treasury agreed to place zero-coupon bonds privately with Brady restructurers to provide them with collateral for their restructured bonds. The US government also used its considerable influence at the IFIs, as well as its connections to its commercial creditors, to urge debt relief via Brady exchanges, including through moral suasion of existing creditors.[78] Today, a similar entity would need to be willing to perform the coordination task to strengthen creditor coordination, urge creditors and debtors to agree to relief, and provide enhancements and other safeguards to induce participation. However, it is unclear whether any country would again be willing to play this role due to domestic political pressure against any actions perceived to be favorable to non-Paris Club creditors. That said, these pressures could be overcome if an appropriate burden sharing of debt relief was achieved, if there were perceived geopolitical benefits (e.g., restructurers overcoming so-called debt-trap

---

[77] See (Horn et al., 2023) and (Watrous, 2024).
[78] The United States paved the way to debt relief by urging its commercial creditors to waive NPCs, for instance, when engaging in Brady exchanges. For more on the United States' role in resolving the 1980s debt crisis, including on the role of the Federal Reserve, see (Sgard, 2023).

diplomacy pushed by non-Paris Club creditors), or if newfound fiscal space could be used to invest in shared goals, such as climate change adaptation and mitigation. More broadly, non-US G7 or emerging creditors could be willing to sponsor the Brady Plan but would likely need the support of the United States for the plan to be a success.[79] Similarly, non-state sponsors could have the balance sheet required to underwrite Brady restructurings but may be similarly constrained by the lack of consensus among key shareholders.

Another operational challenge is the status of guaranteed bonds during restructurings. Recent evidence from Ghana illustrates the difficulty of restructuring a bond with a partial multilateral guarantee (in this case, the World Bank). In this case, the bond included CACs that allowed it to be aggregated in a single pool with non-guaranteed debt (threatening the validity of the guarantee), and did not have effective mechanisms for restructuring the guaranteed versus the unguaranteed portion of the bond. This created challenges for the restructuring process as simply excluding guaranteed bonds from the restructuring perimeter can create issues of inter-creditor equity and entrench the unrealistic expectation that third-party guarantees will never be called (Weidemeyer, Panizza, & Gulati, 2022; Wigglesworth, 2022). More work will need to be done to clarify the role of guaranteed debt in restructurings, especially given the gaining popularity of credit enhancements to ease liquidity strains among borrowers.[80]

Any systemic debt relief initiative would need to think carefully about how to deal with potential holdouts. Buchheit and coworkers describe several carrots that can be used to encourage creditor participation. These inducements include up-front cash; VRIs such as those employed during the Brady era, in which commodity exporters including Mexico, Nigeria, and Venezuela bundled oil price warrants in their restructured debt (with the assumption being that a more favorable oil price outlook would have macro dividends for each of the three listed commodity exporters);[81] loss reinstatement features to hedge against serial defaults; clauses to ensure comparable treatment; and contractual improvements in the restructured debt (Buchheit et al., 2019). Moreover, escrow accounts could be used to induce potential holdouts, in which the debtor pays any interest arrears into an escrow account, committing to reserving the hard currency to pay back the creditor as part of the restructuring. The global

---

[79] Horn and coworkers examine how China has increasingly served as an international lender of last resort via its central bank swap lines (Horn et al., 2023; Watrous, 2024). China's willingness to provide rescue loans, coupled with its considerable global clout, could make it a potential sponsor of a rebooted Brady Plan.

[80] See, for example, the launch of the World Bank's guarantee platform via the Multilateral Investment Guarantee Authority (World Bank, 2024).

[81] More recently, Suriname included oil-linked VRIs in their restructured debt; see (International Monetary Fund, 2023c).

community may also need to discuss potential policy changes related to IMF lending, including potentially reinstating a DDSR policy to support debtors' purchase of set-asides and other financial carrots to boost creditor participation in restructuring processes.[82] Additional policy measures to compensate holdout bilateral creditors could include linking cooperation on debt relief to compromises in other areas, such as on representation at the IFIs (Krueger, 2023).

Sponsors of a new Brady Plan should be willing to develop constructive solutions to the problem of historically low uptake of SCDI and related features. Working with the private sector, common guidelines and rules for pricing SCDIs/VRIs in comparability of treatment and NPV calculations could be developed by groups such as the Paris Club and G20. Additionally, Brady sponsors can work with creditor committees to promote learning and reduce information asymmetries of bonds with embedded options. As was the case during the original Brady Plan, designating market-makers for Brady bonds as a form of compensation for creating a liquid market for the restructured claims could be helpful in enhancing the liquidity of restructured claims including and not including embedded options.

A mix of carrots and sticks could be needed to get reluctant creditors to agree to a restructuring. Sticks include threats of nonpayment; CACs (with the strongest being single-limb aggregate voting, see (Fang, Schumacher, & Trebesch, 2021));[83] changing local laws governing debt repayment to facilitate default; exit consents to reduce the attractiveness of untreated debt; trust structures (i.e., issuing bonds through a trust, which could protect payments from attachment by creditors); and the protection of assets such as via legal immunities (Buchheit et al., 2019).[84]

Debtors would also need to manage the reputational risk of requesting a restructuring, including with the CRAs. Cash and Naidoo claim this *credit rating impasse* may be addressed by suspending credit ratings during the period of negotiation, though it is unclear whether such a suspension is legally feasible (Cash & Naidoo, 2021). While it should be expected that there would be some pushback from creditors and CRAs themselves for such a plan, any systemic debt relief initiative would need to consider how to address the risk of downgrades by CRAs in getting reluctant debtors to request needed (but

---

[82] See IMF (2021a).

[83] Granted, enhanced CACs are most relevant in cases of market-based debt, such as Eurobonds, which are weighted toward vulnerable emerging markets. On the other hand, CACs would be less relevant for LICs that owe debt to the official sector.

[84] On legal immunities, Buchheit and coworkers highlight the example of Iraq from 2005–2008, in which Iraq's assets were shielded from attachment via a United Nations Security Council resolution.

reputationally costly) debt treatments. That said, Brady restructurings could enhance debtors' capacity to repay, which could be credit positive for restructurers.

It is likely that debt restructurings, even in the context of a systemic debt relief initiative, would probably need to remain on a case-by-case basis. Since the 1980s, debt restructuring has proceeded on a case-by-case basis, including in all Brady restructurings. The logic of such an approach is that each debtor is different, and thus each solution to debt distress should be tailored to country-specific circumstances. On the other hand, the increase in common global macroeconomic shocks, coupled with relatively fewer capitalization risks among commercial creditors relative to the 1980s, may favor a more systemic approach. While breakthroughs are possible, achieving consensus on a systemic solution would likely be too contentious and slow, thus biasing the system to favoring a case-by-case approach (Truman, 2020).

Debt operations will continue to require an ex ante assessment about whether a sovereign is experiencing liquidity or solvency challenges, which risk either Type I or Type II errors in debt relief. Liquidity operations attempt to provide near-term debt service relief to the troubled sovereign (e.g., via the DSSI or Baker Plan), while solvency operations seek to restore solvency by reducing the face value of existing debt, with larger haircuts (i.e., the Brady Plan). Ex post economic performance can validate the appropriateness of each ex ante judgment. Trouble emerges either when debt servicing problems are diagnosed as a solvency challenge, when in fact liquidity relief would have restored sustainability (i.e., a Type 1 error, or false positive of the necessity of a Brady treatment), or when liquidity relief is offered while face value write-downs were in fact needed (i.e., a Type 2 error, or false negative, see Figure 42). Worryingly, as mentioned previously, the incentives of official creditors, debtors, and multilateral institutions are often skewed toward making a Type 2 error due to the potential payoff of playing for time.

Hence, debt operations should appropriately balance the risks of Type I and II errors in debt restructuring operations. To hedge against the risks of Type I errors (false positives), creditors could push for restructured bonds to include state-contingent or VRI-style features, which would allow them to share in the upside of restructured debt should subsequent macroeconomic performance exceed estimates made at the time of the restructuring.[85] Local currency debt could fulfill a similar role, as local currency instruments would be expected to perform well in a Type I scenario. Type II errors – situations when liquidity

---

[85] The actual risk of Type I errors in debt restructuring is likely limited, given the tendency of stakeholders to "extend and pretend." On the potential for SCDI use in current debt restructuring cases of Sri Lanka and Zambia, see (Setser, 2023b).

	Ex-ante [1]	
	Liquidity	Solvency
Ex-post Liquidity	Correct	Type I error (false positive)
Ex-post Solvency	Type II error (false negative)	Correct

[1] Debt operations require an ex-ante judgment about whether the sovereign's challenges reflect illiquidity or insolvency.

Figure 42 Managing trade-offs in debt restructuring given uncertainty
Source: Authors

relief is provided when face value write-downs and deeper haircuts are needed to restore sustainability – may require stakeholders to acknowledge the bias toward overoptimistic forecasts while adopting both carrots and sticks to convince reluctant creditors to provide faster and deeper up-front debt relief to troubled sovereigns.

Additional steps to tackle the collective action problem in debt relief could also be taken. The goal of these additional actions would be to reduce the risk of being a first mover requesting a Brady restructuring, raise the reward of going first, while also raising the cost of holding out. Potential options include (1) transparent contingent pledges, in which creditors publicly pledge to underwrite a restructuring only if a certain number of fellow creditors representing a threshold of the total debt stock agree as well; (2) standardized processes and documentation via a menu approach, such as standardizing term sheets and valuation approaches as was the case for the original Brady Plan (see Tables 9 and 10); (3) strong marketing from first movers, including having pilot countries engage in marketing campaigns to distressed sovereigns; and (4) additional inducements for first mover debtors that request debt treatments, such as up-front cash payments.

5.3 Summary

This section argued that Brady-style mechanisms could be useful today, particularly for LICs with bilateral sovereign creditors, but emphasized the need to address novel challenges such as domestic debt and creditor coordination. The section discussed the operational considerations for implementing a twenty-first-century Brady Plan. It highlighted the differences between the current period and the 1980s, such as the more diverse creditor landscape and the tepid global growth outlook. The section stressed the importance of assessing creditor exposure to distressed sovereigns and ensuring that debt write-downs do not cause undue economic harm. It suggested that creditor coordination could be more challenging today due to the larger role of private creditors and non-Paris Club lenders. The section noted that any systemic debt relief initiative would require a willing sponsor, likely a sovereign or international financial institution, to underwrite the plan and provide enhancements to induce participation. It also emphasized the need to manage the reputational risk of requesting a restructuring and to address the potential holdouts through a mix of carrots and sticks. The section concluded that while Brady-style restructurings could offer significant benefits, they would not be a panacea and should be tailored to the specific conditions of distressed sovereigns today. Additionally, the section underscored the importance of balancing the risks of Type I and Type II errors in debt restructuring operations to ensure appropriate and timely relief measures.

6 Conclusions

The purpose of this Element was to assess the macroeconomic impact of the original 1989 Brady Plan and to draw some lessons for debt restructuring in the present period. It argued that the Brady Plan helped achieve fast and durable debt stock reduction for Brady restructurers, with macroeconomic dividends for debtors. Brady-style exchanges led to significant and persistent declines in public and external debt for Brady restructurers relative to the study's control group of EMs. Additionally, Brady restructurers saw broadly better macroeconomic outcomes than their non-Brady peers, including faster economic growth. Taken together, the "multiplier" effect of the face value reductions on debt burdens of the Brady countries was particularly large, which provides prima facie evidence that Brady-style mechanisms can be effective tools for restoring debt sustainability under certain circumstances. This result is broadly consistent with recent research on debt reductions, including as discussed in International Monetary Fund (2023a) and Ando et al. (2023).

Brady exchanges had several features. They allowed for illiquid and non-transparent claims to be converted to marketable securities, with liquidity benefits for creditors and debtors. Brady exchanges also allowed for a diversification of the sovereign creditor base, from commercial banks, which tended to hold debt to maturity, to capital markets, in which there was active buying and selling in the restructured claims. One of the key benefits of the original Brady Plan was strengthening the liquidity of restructured claims while reducing creditor concentration (Miles, 1999).[86] Brady bonds thus opened new categories of institutional investors that would be attracted to the relatively higher returns offered by Brady bonds while still seeking the safety provided by their collateralized structure.[87]

Yet debt relief alone likely does not tell the whole story. Policy commitments achieved through the Brady Plan, including strong country-led ownership of their reform agendas, helped foster macroeconomic sustainability and safeguard reform momentum among debtors. The empirical results of this Element show that Brady restructurers had more favorable outcomes relative to the control group, driven mainly by the sharp pickup in productivity growth. This increase in productivity growth was at least partially attributable to the anchoring of structural reform efforts of Brady countries in the 1990s. IMF programs and macroeconomic stabilization programs likely served as commitment devices of Brady restructurers to undertake needed but potentially difficult-to-implement reforms. As explained previously, Brady restructurers' structural reform effort was stronger than peer countries.[88]

Despite these favorable results, it does not necessarily follow that simply rebooting the original Brady Plan would solve today's debt challenges. For one, Brady exchanges may have worked best because they accompanied deep face value haircuts on sovereign loans that were held to maturity among a relatively more concentrated creditor base of commercial banks. Such large haircuts tend to be required when countries face solvency issues. In cases where liquidity strains are more pressing, such face value reductions may not be required, and thus Brady mechanisms may not be as useful. Still, Brady mechanisms can be useful tools in a diverse toolkit of restructuring options, especially when incumbent creditors would like to enhance the liquidity of their claims, when new features (i.e., SCDIs or tranched structures) could be beneficial, or when country authorities have ambitious reform plans, such that their capacity to repay their restructured claims would be enhanced over time.

Thus, on the policy front, future research can consider how Brady exchanges can complement existing debt restructuring mechanisms today. This Element argued that Brady restructurings helped deliver good outcomes for EMs with a

---

[86] Of course, creditors may need to overcome domestic legal constraints that would hamper their willingness to convert existing bilateral loans into tradeable bonds, such as obtaining parliamentary approval.

[87] This potential benefit is further evidenced by the fact that external sovereign bonds generally offer returns in excess of the compensation for the risk of default, while the same may not necessarily be true for bilateral claims (Meyer, Reinhart, & Trebesch, 2022).

[88] Such improvements in restructurers' institutional contexts and reform momentum are key distinguishing features of Brady restructurings compared to other debt relief efforts, such as HIPC.

strong structural reform effort that had illiquid debts that would benefit from capacity-to-repay assurances (via IMF programs and collateral) and securitization, including for market development. There could be debt restructuring cases for which similar conditions apply today, and in those cases, Brady-style exchanges could be considered. If there existed a demand from both creditors and debtors, it is possible that Brady-style debt restructurings could be incorporated using existing multilateral frameworks, including the CF, which can also be a subject of future work. Future research can also perform more granular assessments of debt vulnerabilities and try to map these modalities to potential qualification in a rebooted Brady Plan, as well as assess how today's more shock-prone and uncertain global conditions may affect the implementation of a new Brady-style mechanism, including by altering the incentives of creditors, debtors, and sponsors differently.

Future academic research could examine why the Brady Plan was relatively more successful than other debt relief initiatives while also employing complementary analytical methods. An additional avenue of future research could compare the Brady Plan and the HIPC debt relief initiative, Multilateral Debt Relief Initiative, and the Vienna Initiative. This research could build on the work done by Arslanalp and Henry (2006), who showed that debt relief alone is not a panacea for growth.[89] Often, the barriers to growth in distressed sovereigns is not principally debt overhang but instead follow from their low institutional quality. Thus, the most likely success stories of debt relief will be countries with a minimum level of institutional quality or those with a willingness to enhance their institutional quality. One avenue of future research could attempt to disambiguate further the relative weights of the drivers of favorable macroeconomic outcomes in Brady restructurers compared to other cases of debt restructuring. Indeed, the present study shows that the suite of reforms and write-downs undertaken and provided via Brady restructurings combined to provide better outcomes than in cases that did not have similar treatments. Additionally, future research can try to extend the political economic analysis of Brady restructurers to understand why their structural reform were stronger than non-Brady countries. In so doing, additional granularity on the types and quality of structural reforms pursued can be obtained. Finally, future research can also employ more case studies of individual Brady countries.

Overall, the future of sovereign debt restructuring will depend on the global macroeconomic landscape, debtors' willingness to pursue macroeconomic and

---

[89] For a recent ex post analysis of HIPC, including on the impact of HIPC on future capital flows from China and other emerging lenders, see (Cordella, Cufre, & Presbitero, 2025).

structural reforms, and the capacity of the global political economy to deliver cooperative results. A higher-for-longer global interest rate environment, coupled with low growth and rising fragmentation, could continue to exacerbate liquidity strains in EMs and LICs, requiring more debt treatments to ease liquidity pressures. Similarly, a sudden global downturn or major drawdown in global asset prices and investor demand for EM and frontier market credit exposure could necessitate a systemic debt relief initiative on the scale of the Brady or HIPC agendas. Critically, the success of any debt relief initiative will hinge on the ability of distressed sovereigns to use their newfound fiscal space both to avoid the fiscal largesse that may have given rise to the need for a debt treatment in the first place, but also to pursue needed reforms to macroeconomic policy frameworks while boosting growth. Finally, debt restructuring is an inherently cooperative exercise, rife with strategic interactions, challenging incentives, potential tensions between the official and private sectors, and a need for strong coordination to overcome these barriers. Ultimately, this cooperative spirit of all major players (or its absence) will determine the future global sovereign debt restructuring. Hopefully, this Element showcases the promise of strong, country-led reforms, innovative thinking, and compromise to deliver growth and prosperity, with lessons for the twenty-first century.

Appendix – Brady Options: Then and Now

Table 10 1980s–1990s Brady menu

Option	Enhancements	Restructured Obligations
Buyback	Up-front cash payment	N/A
Par exchange transaction	Principal prepayment and up to 12% of remaining interest	Securitized with a fixed income stream at about 6.25% or less depending on term structure at time of deal. Generally, a 6.25% coupon payment was less than the prevailing rate on the original debt, thus providing cash flow and NPV relief to the borrower
Discount exchange transaction	Principal prepayment and up to 13% of remaining interest	Securitized with a floating interest stream at LIBOR + 13/16 plus 30–35% face value haircut on the original obligations
Temporary interest reduction exchange	Prepayment of up to 10% of remaining interest	Securitized with a submarket fixed income stream for the first five to six years, followed by a floating interest rate of LIBOR + 13/16 as well as amortization of the principal
Debt conversion/ new money	New loans equal to about 20% of the existing exposure of creditors	Securitized with an interest rate of LIBOR + 7/8 and amortization of principal repayments (based on the original amount).

Source: Clark (1994)

Table 11 Proposed 2020s Brady menu (indicative)

Authors	Option	Enhancements	Restructured Obligations
Buchheit and Lerrick (2023)	Cash down payment structure	Investors receive 30–35% up-front of the bond's current market value	3–3.5% interest rate with twenty-five to thirty-year maturity, amortization of original principal due in the final three years
Buchheit and Lerrick (2023)	Floor of support structure	Collateralized with a zero-coupon World Bank bond	New bond has initial value of 60–70% of bond's current market value, with the minimum value rising to 100% of the nominal amount of the original (i.e., non-restructured) claims at maturity. 3–3.5% interest rate with thirty-five to forty-year maturity
Coulibaly and Abedin (2023)	Recovery and sustainability bonds (RSBs)	RSBs have preferred creditor status and are collateralized by zero-coupon bonds issued by, for example, the World Bank	30% haircut on outstanding private external debt. RSBs have 5% coupon rate with 30-year maturities, with fully amortized principal
Qian (2021)	IFI or sovereign guarantee	IFI guarantees principal and interest rate of collateralized borrowing structure	Restructured bonds have haircuts and SCDI (e.g., commodity)-linked features

Sources: Buchheit and Lerrick (2023); Coulibaly and Abedin (2023); Qian (2021).

Abbreviations

AE	- Advanced economy
CF	- Common Framework for Debt Treatments beyond the Debt Service Suspension Initiative
CRA	- Credit rating agency
DDSR	- Debt and Debt Service Reduction
DDSRO	- Debt- and debt-service reduction operation
DiD	- Difference-in-differences
DSSI	- Debt Service Suspension Initiative
EM	- Emerging market
EMDE	- Emerging markets and developing economy
FIMA	- Foreign and International Monetary Authorities repo facility
GSDR	- Global Sovereign Debt Roundtable
HIPC	- Heavily Indebted Poor Country Initiative
IDA	- International Development Association
IFI	- International financial institution
IMF	- International Monetary Fund
LIC	- Low-income country
MONA	- Monitoring of Fund Arrangements database
MYRA	- Multi-year rescheduling agreements
NIIP	- Net international investment position
NPC	- Negative pledge clause
NPV	- Net present value
OSI	- Official sector involvement
PCS	- Preferred creditor status
PRGT	- IMF's Poverty Reduction and Growth Trust
PSI	- Private sector involvement
PWT	- Penn World Table
QPC	- Quantitative performance criteria (IMF programs)
RSBs	- Recovery and Sustainability Bonds
SCDI	- State-contingent debt instrument
SCM	- Synthetic control method
SDR	- Special Drawing Right
SLA	- Staff-Level Agreement
TFP	- Total factor productivity
UCT	- Upper-credit tranche

References

Abadie, A., & Gardeazabal, J. (2003). The Economic Costs of Conflict: A Case Study of the Basque Country. *American Economic Review, 93*(1), 112–132.

Abadie, A., Diamond, A., & Hainmueller, J. (2010). Synthetic Control Methods for Comparative Case Studies: Estimating the Effect of California's Control Program. *Journal of the American Statistical Association, 105*(490), 493–505.

Adhikari, B., & Alm, J. (2016). Evaluating the Economic Effects of Flat Tax Reforms Using Synthetic Control Methods. *Southern Economic Journal, 83*(2), 437–463.

Adhikari, B., Duval, R. A., Hu, B., & Loungani, P. (2016). Can Reform Waves Turn the Tide? Some Case Studies Using the Synthetic Control Method. *IMF Working Papers, 16*(171), 1–35.

Ahmed, M., & Brown, H. (2022, January 18). *Fix the Common Framework for Debt before It Is Too Late*. Center for Global Development. www.cgdev.org/blog/fix-common-framework-debt-it-too-late.

Aiyar, S., Ilyina, A., & Others. (2023). Geo-economic Fragmentation and the Future of Multilateralism. *IMF Staff Discussion Note*, 1–37.

Alesina, A., Azzalini, G., Favero, C., Giavazzi, F., & Miano, A. (2016). Is It the "How" or the "When" that Matters in Fiscal Adjustments? *NBER Working Papers*, 22863.

Alfaro, L. (2015). Sovereign Debt Restructuring: Evaluating the Impact of the Argentina Ruling. *Harvard Business Law Review, 5*(1), 47–72.

Ando, Sakai and Asonuma, Tamon and Mishra, Prachi and Sollaci, Alexandre, Sovereign Debt Restructuring and Reduction in Debt-to-GDP Ratio (May 06, 2025).

Anderson, J., & Leeper, E. M. (2023). A Fiscal Accounting of COVID Inflation. *Mercatus Special Study, Mercatus Center at George Mason University*, 1–34.

Arslanalp, S., & Eichengreen, B. (2023). Living with High Public Debt. *Jackson Hole Economic Symposium* (pp. 1–45). Jackson Hole: Federal Reserve Bank of Kansas City.

Arslanalp, S., & Henry, P. B. (2005). Is Debt Relief Efficient? *The Journal of Finance, 60*(2), 1017–1051.

Arslanalp, S., & Henry, P. B. (2006). Policy Watch: Debt Relief. *Journal of Economic Perspectives, 20*(1), 207–220.

Asonuma, T., & Trebesch, C. (2016). Sovereign Debt Restructurings: Preemptive or Post-default. *Journal of the European Economic Association, 14*(1), 175–214.

Asonuma, T., Chamon, M., Erce, A., & Sasahara, A. (2019). Costs of Sovereign Defaults: Restructuring Strategies, Bank Distress and the Capital Inflow-Credit Channe. *IMF Working Papers* (69), 1–91.

Baker, A., Larcker, D. F., & Wang, C. C. (2021). How Much Should We Trust Staggered Difference-in-Differences Estimates? *Harvard Business School Working Papers* 21–112, 1–69.

Baqir, R., Ramcharan, R., & Sahay, R. (2005). IMF Programs and Growth: Is Optimism Defensible? *IMF Staff Papers*, 52(2), 260–286.

Beaudry, P., & Willems, T. (2022). On the Macroeconomic Consequences of Over-Optimism. *American Economic Review*, 14(1), 38–59.

Beaumont, C., & Hakura, D. (2021). *The Common Framework: Utilizing Its Flexibility to Support Developing Countries' Recovery*. Washington, DC: International Monetary Fund.

Becker, B., & Ivashina, V. (2014). Reaching for Yield in the Bond Market. *The Journal of Finance*, 70(5), 1863–1902.

Benjamin, D., & Wright, M. L. (2019). Deconstructing Delays in Sovereign Debt Restructuring. *Oxford Economics Papers*, 71(2), 382–404.

Berthélemy, J.-C., & Lensink, R. (1992). An Assessment of the Brady Plan Agreements. *OECD Development Center*, 67, 1–44.

Best, T., Bush, O., Eyraud, L., & Sbrancia, M. B. (2019). Reducing Debt Short of Default. In S. A. Abbas, A. Pienkowski, & K. Rogoff, eds., *Sovereign Debt: A Guide for Economistsand Practitioners* (pp. 225–274). Oxford: Oxford University Press.

Bi, R., Chamon, M., & Zettelmeyer, J. (2016). The Problem that Wasn't: Coordination Failures in Sovereign Debt Restructurings. *IMF Economic Review*, 64, 471–501.

Billmeier, A., & Nannicini, T. (2013). Assessing Economic Liberalization Episodes: A Synthetic Control Approach. *The Review of Economics and Statistics*, 95(3), 983–1001.

Blanchard, O. (2023). *Fiscal Policy under Low Interest Rates*. Cambridge, MA: MIT Press.

Blinder, A. S. (2022). *A Monetary and Fiscal History of the United States, 1961–2021*. Princeton, NJ: Princeton University Press.

Bogdanowicz-Bindert, C. A. (1986). The Debt Crisis: The Baker Plan Revisited. *Journal of Interamerican Studies and World Affairs*, 28(3), 33–45.

Bolhuis, M. A., Chen, J., & Kett, B. R. (2023). Fragmentation in Global Trade: Accounting for Commodities. *IMF Working Papers* (73), 1–35.

Bordo, M. D. (1992). The Bretton Woods International Monetary Syste: An Historical Overview. *NBER Working Paper Series* 4033, 1–148.

Born, B., Müller, G., Schularick, M., & Sedlacek, P. (2019). The Costs of Economic Nationalism: Evidence from the Brexit Experiment. *The Economic Journal*, *129*(623), 2722–2744.

Bräutigam, D. (2023). The Developing World's Coming Debt Crisis. *Foreign Affairs*. https://www.foreignaffairs.com/china/developing-worlds-coming-debt-crisis

Bräutigam, D. A., & Huang, Y. (2023). Integrating China into Multilateral Debt Relief: Progress and Problems in the G20 DSSI. *China Africa Research Initiative (CARI)*, *2023*(9), 1–71.

Bretton Woods Project. (2022, December 8). *Chad Gets Debt Rescheduling, Not Relief, and Is Left Dependent on Oil Revenues*. www.brettonwoodsproject.org/2022/12/chad-gets-debt-rescheduling-not-relief-and-is-left-dependent-on-oil-revenues/.

Brunnermeier, M., Merkel, S., & Sannikov, Y. (2020). The Fiscal Theory of the Price Level with a Bubble. *National Bureau of Economic Research* 27116.

Buchheit, L. C., & Gulati, M. (2020). Avoiding a Lost Decade – Sovereign Debt Workouts in the Post-covid Era. *Capital Markets Law Journal*, *16*(1), 45–55.

Buchheit, L. C., & Lerrick, A. (2023). A Modern Template for the Restructuring of Poor Country Debts. *Capital Markets Law Journal* 18(2), 194–201.

Buchheit, L., Chabert, G., DeLong, C., & Zettelmeyer, J. (2019). The Restructuring Process. In S. A. Abbas, A. Pienkowski, & K. Rogoff, eds., *Sovereign Debt: A Guide for Economists and Practitioners* (pp. 328–364). Oxford: Oxford University Press.

Buiter, W. (2025). Central Banks as Fiscal and Financial Agents of the State. *CEPR Discussion Paper Series*, 1–23.

Calleo, D. P. (1981). Inflation and American Power. *Foreign Affairs*, 781–812.

Campos, R., Do Rosario, J., & Kuipers, A. (2023, May 4). *Suriname Reaches Debt Restructuring Deal with Bondholders*. Reuters. www.reuters.com/markets/suriname-bondholders-reach-debt-restructuring-deal-sources-2023-05-03/#:~:text=A%20value%20recovery%20instrument%20linked,%2C%22%20said%20the%20government%20statement.

Carnot, N. (2013, April). The Composition of Fiscal Adjustments: Some Principles. *ECFIN Economic Brief* (23), 1–6.

Cash, D., & Naidoo, R. (2021). Understanding the Effects of the "Credit Rating". *The Credit Rating Research Initiative*, 1–67.

Chabert, G., Cerisola, M., & Hakura, D. (2022, April 7). *Restructuring Debt of Poorer Nations Requires More Efficient Coordination*. IMF.org. https://meetings.imf.org/en/IMF/Home/Blogs/Articles/2022/04/07/restructuring-debt-of-poorer-nations-requires-more-efficient-coordination.

Chuku, C., Samal, P., Saito, J. et al. (2023). Are We Heading for Another Debt Crisis in Low-Income Countries? Debt Vulnerabilities: Today vs. the Pre-HIPC Era. *IMF Working Papers*, *23*(79), 1–41.

Clark, J. (1994). Debt Reduction and Market Reentry under the Brady Plan. *FRBNY Quarterly Review*, 38–62.

Cline, W. R. (1995). *International Debt Reexamined*. Washington, DC: Institute for International Economics.

Cochrane, J. H. (2022). Fiscal Histories. *Journal of Economic Perspectives*, *36* (4), 125–146.

Corbett, M. (2013, November 22). *Oil Shock of 1973–74*. Federal Reserve History. www.federalreservehistory.org/essays/oil-shock-of-1973-74.

Cordella, T., Cufre, M., & Presbitero, A. F. (2025). The HIPC Initiaitive and China's Emergence as a Lender: Post Hoc or Propter Hoc. *IMF Working Papers, 2025* (33), 1–23.

Coulibaly, B. S., & Abedin, W. (2023). Addressing the Looming Sovereign Debt Crisis in the Developing World: It Is Time to Consider a "Brady Plan." *Global Economy and Development at Brookings*, 1–15.

Crosignani, M. (2021). Bank Capital, Government Bond Holdings, and Sovereign Debt Capacity. *Journal of Financial Economics*, *141*(2), 693–704.

Cruces, J. J., & Trebesch, C. (2013). Sovereign Defaults: The Price of Haircuts. *American Economic Journal: Macroeconomics* 5 (3), 85–117.

Debrun, X., Ostry, J. D., Willems, T., & Wyplosz, C. (2020). Debt Sustainability. In S. Abbas, A. Pienkowski, & K. Rogoff, eds., *Sovereign Debt: A Guide for Economists and Practitioners* (pp. 151–191). Oxford: Oxford University Press.

Dielmann, C. (2021). *On Free-Riders and Sovereign Default: The Rise of Non-traditional Bilateral Lenders and the Resulting Challenges to International Debt Renegotiations*. Baltimore, MD: Johns Hopkins University.

Easterly, W. (2002). *The Elusive Quest for Growth: Economists' Adventures and Misadventures in the Tropics*. Cambridge, MA: MIT Press.

Economides, N., & Smith, R. C. (2011). Trichet Bonds to Resolve the European Sovereign Debt Problem. *NET Institute Working Papers*, *11*(1), 1–7.

Eichengreen, B., & Hausmann, R. (1999). Exchange Rates and Financial Fragility. *New Challenges for Monetary Policy* (pp. 319–367). Jackson Hole, WY: Federal Reserve Bank of Kansas City Jackson Hole symposium.

EMTA. (2022). *Trade Association for the Emerging Markets*. The Brady Plan. www.emta.org/em-background/the-brady-plan/.

Essers, D., & Ide, S. (2019). The IMF and Precautionary Lending: An Empirical Evaluation of the Selectivity and Effectiveness of the Flexible Credit Line. *Journal of International Money and Finance*, *92*(C), 25–61.

Fang, C., Schumacher, J., & Trebesch, C. (2021). Restructuring Sovereign Bonds: Holdouts, Haircuts, and the Effectiveness of CACs. *IMF Economic Review*, *69*, 155–196.

Farah-Yacoub, J., Graf von Luckner, C., & Grund, S. (2025). The International Financial Architecture and Sovereign Debt Crisis Resolution. *Routledge Handbook of International Economic Law* 26, 402–422. https://www.routledge.com/Routledge-Handbook-on-International-Economic-Law/Collins-Vadi/p/book/9781032507972.

Feenstra, R. C., Inklaar, R., & Timmer, M. P. (2015). The Next Generation of the Penn World Table. *American Economic Review*, *105*(10), 3150–3182.

Fitch Ratings. (2021, February 16). *Common Framework Access Could Lead to Sovereign Debt Default*. www.fitchratings.com/research/sovereigns/common-framework-access-could-lead-to-sovereign-debt-default-16-02-2021.

Furman, J., & Summers, L. (2020). *A Reconsideration of Fiscal Policy in the Era of Low Interest Rates*. Washington, DC: Brookings Institution.

Gaspar, V., Poplawski-Ribiero, M., & Yoo, J. (2023, September 13). *Global Debt Is Returning to Its Rising Trend*. IMF.org. www.imf.org/en/Blogs/Articles/2023/09/13/global-debt-is-returning-to-its-rising-trend.

George, L. (2023, June 20). *Analysis: Common Framework, Familiar Problems: Hopes of Debt Breakthrough Fade*. Reuters. www.reuters.com/business/finance/common-framework-familiar-problems-hopes-debt-breakthrough-fade-2023-06-20/.

Georgieva, K. (2022, October 14). *The IMF's Role in a More Shock-Prone World*. IMF.org. www.imf.org/en/News/Articles/2022/10/14/sp101422-imf-managing-director-speech-to-the-plenary-meeting.

Georgieva, K. (2023, July 18). *IMF Managing Director Kristalina Georgieva Urges G20 Leadership to Strengthen the Global Financial Safety Net*. IMF.org. www.imf.org/en/News/Articles/2023/07/18/pr23263-imf-md-georgieva-urges-g20-leadership-to-strengthen-the-global-financial-safety-net?cid=em-COM-789-46943.

Georgieva, K., & Pazarbasioglu, C. (2021, December 2). *The G20 Common Framework for Debt Treatments Must Be Stepped Up*. IMF.org. www.imf.org/en/Blogs/Articles/2021/12/02/blog120221the-g20-common-framework-for-debt-treatments-must-be-stepped-up.

Ghosh, A. R., Kim, J. I., Mendoza, E. G., Ostry, J. D., & Qureshi, M. S. (2013). Fiscal Fatigue, Fiscal Space and Debt Sustainability in Advanced Economies. *The Economic Journal*, *123*(566), F4–F30.

Global Sovereign Debt Roundtable. (2024). *Compendium of GSDR Common Understanding on Technical Issues*.

Global Sovereign Debt Roundtable. (2025). *Sovereign Debt Restructuring: A Playbook for Country Authorities*. Washington, DC.

Gopinath, G. (2023, December 11). *Cold War II? Preserving Economic Cooperation Amid Geoeconomic Fragmentation*. IMF.org. www.imf.org/en/News/Articles/2023/12/11/sp121123-cold-war-ii-preserving-economic-cooperation-amid-geoeconomic-fragmentation.

Graefe, L. (2013, November 22). *Oil Shock of 1978–79*. Federal Reserve History. www.federalreservehistory.org/essays/oil-shock-of-1978-79#:~:text=Oil%20prices%20began%20to%20rise,of%20oil%20during%20the%20crisis.

Grigorian, D. A. (2023, February 13). *Restructuring Domestic Sovereign Debt: Fiscal Savings and Financial Stability Considerations*. Brookings.edu.www.brookings.edu/articles/restructuring-domestic-sovereign-debt-fiscal-savings-and-financial-stability/.

Grogorian, D. A., & Vessereau, L. (2024, December). Ghana: A Case Study of Sovereign Debt Restructuring under the G20 Common Framework. *Center for Global Development Working Papers* 710, 1–24.

Gumbau-Brisa, F., & Mann, C. L. (2009). Reviving Mortgage Securitizatoin: Lessons from the Brady Plan and Duration Analysis. *Federal Reserve Bank of Boston Public Policy Discussion Papers* 09-3, 1–49.

Guzman, M., Ocampo, J., & Stiglitz, J. E. (2016). *Too Little, Too Late: The Quest to Resolve Sovereign Debt Crises*. New York: Columbia University Press.

Hagan, S. (2020). Sovereign Debt Restructuring: The Centrality of the IMF's Role. *Peterson Institute for International Economics Working Paper* 20-13, 1–14.

Hagan, S. (2022, September 28). *The IMF's Arrears Lending Policy: Just Use It*. Financial Times. www.ft.com/content/8b9340a5-b4ca-4e1f-b4b7-cb5003fdb27e.

Hagan, S., & Setser, B. W. (2024, May). Restructuring Sovereign Debt: The Need for a Coordinated Framework. *Peterson Institute for International Economics Policy Brief*, *23*(4), 1–14.

Hakura, D. (2020). What Is Debt Sustainability? *Finance & Development*, 60–61.

Henning, C. R. (2023). How to Make Sovereign Debt Restructuring Work Now. *Centre for International Governance Innovation*(179), 1–12.

Horn, S., Parks, B. C., Reinhart, C. M., & Trebesch, C. (2023). China as an International Lender of Last Resort. *NBER Working Paper Series*(31105), 1–40.

Holland, A. & Pazarbasioglu, P. (2024, January 24). *How to Ease Rising External Debt-Service Pressures in Low-Income Countries*. International

Monetary Fund. www.imf.org/en/Blogs/Articles/2024/01/24/how-to-ease-rising-external-debt-service-pressures-in-low-income-countries.

Huang, Y., & Bräutigam, D. (2025). Socialisation, Policy Opportunity, and Bureaucratic Bargaining: Explaining China's Zig-Zag Engagement with Multilateral Debt Restructuring. *Review of International Political Economy* 32 (4), 1–25.

International Monetary Fund. (2013). *Sovereign Debt Restructuring-Recent Developments and Implications for the Fund's Legal and Policy Framework.* Washington, DC.

International Monetary Fund. (2017). *State-Contingent Debt Instruments for Sovereigns.* Washington, DC.

International Monetary Fund. (2020a). *The International Architecture for Resolving Sovereign Debt Involving Private-Sector Creditors–Recent Developments, Challenges, and Reform Options.* Washington, DC.

International Monetary Fund. (2020b). The Role of State-Contingent Debt Instruments in Sovereign Debt Restructurings. *International Monetary Fund Staff Discussion Notes*, 1–34.

International Monetary Fund. (2021a). Fund Support for Debt- and Debt-Service-Reduction Operations. *IMF Policy Paper*, 1–41.

International Monetary Fund. (2021b). *Issues in Restructuring of Soevereign Domestic Debt.* Washington, DC.

International Monetary Fund. (2022a). *Staff Guidance Note on the Sovereign Risk and Debt Sustainability Framework for Market Access Countries.* Washington, DC.

International Monetary Fund. (2022b). *IMF Annual Report.* Debt Dynamics.

International Monetary Fund. (2023a). *World Economic Outlook: A Rocky Recovery.* Washington, DC.

International Monetary Fund. (2023b). *Global Financial Stability Report.* Washington, DC.

International Monetary Fund. (2023c). *Suriname: Second Review under the Extended Arrangement under the Extended Fund Facility.* Washington, DC.

International Monetary Fund. (2023d). *World Economic Outlook: Navigating Global Divergences.* Washington, DC.

International Monetary Fund. (2024a). *Policy Reform Proposals to Promote the Fund's Capacity to Support Countries Undertaking Debt Restructuring.* Washington, DC.

International Monetary Fund. (2024b). *Guidance Note on the Financing Assurances and Sovereign Arrears Policies and the Fund's Role in Debt Restructurings.* Washington, DC.

International Monetary Fund. (2025a). *The 4th Financing for Development Conference-Contribution of the IMF to the International Financing for Development Agenda*. Washington, DC.

International Monetary Fund. (2025b, January 17). *IMF Executive Board Completes the Second Review under the Extended Credit Facility (ECF) Arrangement for Ethiopia*. www.imf.org/en/News/Articles/2025/01/17/pr25006-ethiopia-imf-executive-board-completes-second-review-ecf-arrangement.

International Monetary Fund. (n.d.). *Catastrophe Containment and Relief Trust*. www.imf.org/en/About/Factsheets/Sheets/2023/Catastrophe-containment-relief-trust-CCRT.

International Monetary Fund and World Bank. (2024). *IMF-World Bank Non-paper on Actions to Support Countries Faced with Liquidity Challenges*. Washington, DC.

Irwin, D. A. (2012). The Nixon Shock after Forty Years: The Import Surcharge Revisited. *NBER Working Papers* (17749).

Irwin, D. A., & Obstfeld, M. (2024). *Floating Exchange Rates at Fifty*. Washington, DC: Peterson Institute for International Economics.

Joyce, J. P. (2025). *International Investment Income*. Cambridge: Cambridge University Press.

Kelton, S. (2020). *The Deficit Myth: Modern Monetary Theory and the Birth of the People's Economy*. New York: Public Affairs.

Kose, M. A., Ohnsorge, F. L., Reinhart, C. M., & Rogoff, K. S. (2022). The Aftermath of Debt Surges. *Annual Review of Economics*, *14*, 637–663.

Krueger, A. O. (2023, April 17). *Breaking the Debt-Relief Paralysis*. Project Syndicate. www.project-syndicate.org/commentary/imf-china-international-debt-restructuring-process-is-broken-by-anne-o-krueger-2023-04.

Kuruc, K. (2022). Are IMF Rescue Packages Effective? A Synthetic Control Analysis of Macroeconomic Crises. *Journal of Monetary Economics*, *127* (C), 38–53.

Lane, P. R., & Milesi-Ferretti, G. (2018). The External Wealth of Nations Revisited: International Financial Integration in the Aftermath of the Global Financial Crisis. *IMF Economic Review*, *66*, 189–222.

Lang, V., Mihalyi, D., & Presbitero, A. F. (2023). Borrowing Costs after Sovereign Debt Relief. *American Economic Journal* 15(2), 331–358.

Lazard. (2025a). *The 2020–2025 Sovereign Debt Crisis: What Have We Learnt and What Lies Ahead?*

Lazard. (2025b). *The Preferred Creditor Status Glut – The Search for Loss Absorption in Africa*.

Loungani, P., Mate, A., McCarthy, M., & Collodel, U. (2023). The IMF's Forecasting and Policy Advice Formulation Processes during the Pandemic. *IEO Background Paper*, 1–42.

Makoff, G. (2024). *Default: The Landmark Court Battle over Argentina's $100 Billion Debt Restructuring*. Washington, DC: Georgetown University Press.

Makoff, G., Maret, T., & Wright, L. (2025). *Sovereign Debt Restructuring with China at the Table: Forward Progress but Lost Decade Risk Remains*. Harvard Kennedy School. Cambridge, MA: Harvard Kennedy School Mossavar-Rahmani Center for Business and Government.

Malpass, D. (2022). *Remarks by World Bank Group President David Malpass at the 2022 Spring Meetings: "Making Debt Work for Development."* Washington, DC: The World Bank Group.

Malpass, D. (2023, April 26). *Remarks by World Bank Group President David Malpass at the Breaking the Impasse on Global Debt Restructurings Conference*. World Bank. www.worldbank.org/en/news/speech/2023/04/26/malpass-president-breaking-impasse-global-debt-restructurings-conference.

Martha, R. S. (1990). Preferred Creditor Status under International Law: The Case of the International Monetary Fund. *International and Comparative Law Quarterly*, *39*(4), 801–826.

Mbaye, S., Moreno Badia, M., & Chae, K. (2018). Global Debt Database: Methodology and Sources. *IMF Working Papers*, *18*(111), 1–52.

Mendelowitz, A. I. (1990, August 14). Treasury's Sale of Zero-Coupon Bonds to Mexico. Washington, DC: USA.

Meyer, J., Reinhart, C. M., & Trebesch, C. (2022). Sovereign Bonds since Waterloo. *NBER Working Paper Series* (25543).

Miles, W. (1999). Securitization, Liquidity, and the Brady Plan. *The North American Journal of Economics and Finance*, *10*(2), 423–442.

Monteagudo, M. (1994). The Debt Problem: The Baker Plan and the Brady Initiative: A Latin American. *The International Lawyer*, *28*(1), 59–81.

Nannicini, T., & Billmeier, A. (2011). Economies in Transition: How Important Is Trade Openness for Growth? *Oxford Bulletin of Economics and Statistics*, *73*(3), 287–314.

Neiman, B. (2022, September 20). *Remarks by Counselor to the Secretary of the Treasury Brent Neiman at the Peterson Institute for International Economics*. Treasury.gov. https://home.treasury.gov/news/press-releases/jy0963.

Neiman, B. (2023, October 23). *Remarks by Assistant Secretary of Treasury for International Finance Brent Neiman at Johns Hopkins School for Advanced International Studies*. Treasury.gov. https://home.treasury.gov/news/press-releases/jy1833.

Newiak, M., & Willems, T. (2017). Evaluating the Impact of Non-Financial IMF Programs Using the Synthetic Control Method. *IMF Working Papers*, *17* (109), 1–43.

Ocampo, J. A. (2017). *Resetting the International Monetary (Non)System*. Oxford: Oxford University Press.

Ostry, J. D., Ghosh, A. R., Kim, J. I., & Qureshi, M. S. (2010). Fiscal Space. *IMF Staff Position Note*, *10*(11), 1–25.

Panizza, U. (2024). The Pitfalls of Value Recovery Instruments in Sovereign Debt Restructuring. *Finance for Development Lab Policy Note*, 1–17.

Pazarbasioglu, C. (2024). *Sovereign Debt Restructuring Process Is Improving Amid Cooperation and Reform*. Washington, DC: International Monetary Fund.

Pitchford, R., & Wright, M. L. (2010). Holdouts in Sovereign Debt Restructuring: A Theory of Negotiation in a Weak Contractual Environment. *NBER Working Paper Series* (16632), 1–40.

Politico EU. (2024, February 20). *It's Time to Cancel Debt for Climate-Stricken Nations, Barbados Leader Says*. www.politico.eu/article/cancel-debt-climate-change-barbados-mia-mottley/.

Qian, Y. (2021). Brady Bonds and the Potential for Debt Restructuring in the Post-Pandemic Era. *BU Global Development Policy Center Working Papers* (9), 1–23.

Rogoff, K. (2022). Emerging Market Sovereign Debt in the Aftermath of the Pandemic. *Journal of Economic Perspectives*, *36*(4), 147–166.

Reinhart, Carmen M., Vincent Reinhart, and Christoph Trebesch. 2016. "Global Cycles: Capital Flows, Commodities, and Sovereign Defaults, 1815-2015." *American Economic Review* 106 (5): 574–80.

Rojas-Suárez, L., & Weisbrod, S. R. (1996). Managing Banking Crises in Latin America: The Do's and Don'ts of Successful Bank Restructuring Programs. *IADB Working Papers*, 1–30.

Sarkar, A. U. (1994). Debt Relief for Environment: Experience and Issues. *The Journal of Environment & Development*, *3*(1), 123–136.

Schuknecht, L. (2022). *Debt Sustainability: A Global Perspective*. Cambridge: Cambridge University Press.

Setser, B. (2023a, March 26). *The Common Framework and Its Discontents*. Council on Foreign Relations. www.cfr.org/blog/common-framework-and-its-discontents.

Setser, B. (2023b, May 3). *Getting Debt Restructuring Terms Right*. Council on Foreign Relations. www.cfr.org/blog/getting-debt-restructuring-terms-right.

Setser, B. W. (2024, January 12). *@Brad_Setser*. X.com. https://x.com/Brad_Setser/status/1745877661140824076.

Setser, B. W. (2025). Focusing the IMF's Role in Development Finance on Debt Sustainability. *ICE, Rivista de Economía*, 37–48.

Sgard, J. (2023). *The Debt Crisis of the 1980s*. Cheltenham: Edward Elgar.

Shalal, A. (2023, April 25). *World Bank Chief Economist Gill Calls for New Approaches to Address "Debt Crisis."* Reuters. https://infodisplay.infodesk.com/item/c6b7e31f-4f30-4f21-a423-ffc54c2ef1ea.html?CU=imf5992&APP=6.

Sims, J., & Romero, J. (2013, November 22). *Latin American Debt Crisis of the 1980s: 1982–1989*. Federal Reserve History. www.federalreservehistory.org/essays/latin-american-debt-crisis.

Skidmore, T. E., Smith, P. H., & Green, J. N. (2010). *Modern Latin America (7th Ed)*. Oxford: Oxford Univerisity Press.

Sobel, M. (2016). Strengthening Collective Action Clauses: Catalysing Change – The Back Story. *Capital Markets Law Journal*, *11*(1), 3–11.

Sobel, M. (2022, August 16). Sovereign Debt Architecture Is Messy and Here to Stay: Deal with It. *Financial Times*.

Steil, B. (2018). *The Marshall Plan: Dawn of the Cold War*. New York: Simon & Schuster.

Sturzenegger, F., & Zettelmeyer, J. (2006). *Debt Defaults and Lessons from a Decade of Crises*. Cmabride, MA: MIT Press.

Talero, B. X. (2022). Potential Statutory Options to Encourage Private Sector Creditor Participation in the Common Framework. *World Bank – Equitable Growth, Finance & Institutions Notes*, 1–13.

The Group of Thirty. (2020). *Sovereign Debt and Financing for Recovery*. Washington, DC.

Trebesch, C., Meyer, J., Reinhart, C., & Grav von Luckner, C. (2021, March 30). *External Sovereign Debt Restructurings: Delay and Replay*. VoxEU.

Truman, E. M. (2020). Sovereign Debt Relief in the Global Pandemic: Lessons from the 1980s. *Peterson Institute for International Economics Working Papers*, 1–11.

United Nations. (2022, March 21). *Credit Rating Agencies and Sovereign Debt: Challenges and Solutions*. UN.org. www.un.org/development/desa/financing/document/credit-rating-agencies-and-sovereign-debt-challenges-and-solutions.

United Press International. (1990, August 15). *GAO Says Mexico Got a Subsidy from Bond Sale: Finance: The Watchdog Agency Says the Latin Nation Got a $192-Million Break in Its Debt. The Treasury Department Disputes the Charge*. LA Times Archives. www.latimes.com/archives/la-xpm-1990-08-15-fi-541-story.html.

Vásquez, I. (1996). The Brady Plan and Market-Based Solutions to Debt Crises. *Cato Journal, 16*(2), 233–243.

Vatican News. (2025, January 1). *Pope Calls on World Leaders to Cancel Debt of Poorer Nations*. www.vaticannews.va/en/pope/news/2025-01/pope-calls-on-world-leaders-to-cancel-debt-of-poorer-nations.html#:~:text=After%20his%20traditional%20New%20Years,debts%20of%20the%20poorest%20countries.%E2%80%9D

Virketis, P. (2024). *The Product of All Fears: IMF's USD GDP Forecast Quality during EM Bond Restructurings*. HBK.

Watrous, J. (2024). *New Lenders of Last Resort: Bilateral Bailouts and IMF Conditionality*. London: London School of Economics.

Weber, A. (2012). Stock-Flow Adjustments and Fiscal Transparency: A Cross-Country Comparison. *IMF Working Papers* (39), 1–19.

Weidemeyer, M., Panizza, U., & Gulati, M. (2022, November 29). *FUD and the Ghana 2030 Bond: When Guarantees Lead to a Guaranteed Headache*. Financial Times. www.ft.com/content/fa3fddbf-72a7-475d-81f3-22bb68caaea6.

Wigglesworth, R. (2022, November 30). *The World Bank's Guarantee Debacles: Aventures in Super-Seniority*. Financial Times. www.ft.com/content/34f1198c-6d36-4328-816a-e30a85ada6d7.

Wigglesworth, R., & Yu, S. (2023, April 13). *How China Changed the Game for Countries in Default*. Financial Times. www.ft.com/content/19add278-aa83-45f8-a84f-12750f32258f.

Wolf, M. (2008). *Fixing Global Finance*. Baltimore, MD: Johns Hopkins University Press.

Wolf, M. (2022, January 17). *We Must Tackle the Looming Global Debt Crisis before It's Too Late*. Financial Times. www.ft.com/content/889fec5a-cb62-463f-af8c-22c841bddb65.

World Bank. (2022a, February 28). *Debt Service Suspension Initiative*. Worldbank.org. www.worldbank.org/en/topic/debt/brief/covid-19-debt-service-suspension-initiative.

World Bank. (2022b). *International Debt Report: Updated International Debt Statistics*. Washington, DC.

World Bank. (2022c). *Resolving High Debt after the Pandemic: Lessons from Past Episodes of Debt Relief*. Washington, DC.

World Bank. (2024, April 11). *New Guarantee Platform Delivers Efficiency, Simplicity to Boost Impact*. Worldbank.org. www.worldbank.org/en/news/feature/2024/04/11/new-guarantee-platform-delivers-efficiency-simplicity-to-boost-impact.

Yellen, J. (2023a, April 20). *Remarks by Secretary of the Treasury Janet L. Yellen on the US–China Economic Relationship at Johns Hopkins*

School of Advanced International Studies. Treasury.gov. https://home.treasury.gov/news/press-releases/jy1425.

Yellen, J. (2023b, July 8). *Remarks by Secretary of the Treasury Janet L. Yellen at Press Conference in Beijing, the People's Republic of China*. Treasury.gov. https://home.treasury.gov/news/press-releases/jy1603.

Yellen, J. (2023c, July 16). *Remarks by Secretary of the Treasury Janet L. Yellen at Press Conference in Gandhinagar, India*. Treasury.gov. https://home.treasury.gov/news/press-releases/jy1617.

Acknowledgments

The authors would like to thank Ceyla Pazarbasioglu for her overall guidance of this project, as well as Anteneh Addisu, Serkan Arslanalp, Tamon Asonuma, Mary Chaves, Emmanuel Comolet, Jesse Corradi, Chanda DeLong, Christopher Dielmann, Mark Flanagan, Sean Hagan, Tara Hariharan, Allison Holland, Henry Hoyle, Robert Powell, Federico Sequeda, Mark Sobel, Arthur Sode, Tao Tan, Tim Willems, and Robert Zoellick for their comments. They are also grateful for the helpful conversations on fiscal policy and sovereign debt with Sascha Buetzer, Guillaume Chabert, Rex Ghosh, David Malpass, Geoffrey Okamoto, Rahul Rekhi, and Mark Rosen. They thank Paula Arias, Yue Chang, and Shiming Xiong for their excellent research assistance. The authors also thank Kenneth Reinert for his support for this project and appreciate the constructive feedback received from two anonymous peer reviewers. The views expressed are strictly those of the authors and do not necessarily represent the views of the IMF, its Executive Board, or management. All remaining errors are the authors' alone.

Cambridge Elements

International Economics

Kenneth A. Reinert
George Mason University

Kenneth A. Reinert is Professor of Public Policy in the Schar School of Policy and Government at George Mason University where he directs the Global Commerce and Policy master's degree program. He is author of *An Introduction to International Economics: New Perspectives on the World Economy* with Cambridge University Press and coauthor of *Globalization for Development: Meeting New Challenges* with Oxford University Press. He is also editor of *The Handbook of Globalisation and Development* with Edward Elgar and co-editor of the two-volume *Princeton Encyclopedia of the World Economy* with Princeton University Press.

About the Series

International economics is a distinct field with both fundamental theoretical insights and increasing empirical and policy relevance. The *Cambridge Elements in International Economics* showcases this field, covering the subfields of international trade, international money and finance, and international production, and featuring both established researchers and new contributors from all parts of the world. It aims for a level of theoretical discourse slightly above that of the *Journal of Economic Perspectives* to maintain accessibility. It extends Cambridge University Press' established reputation in international economics into the new, digital format of *Cambridge Elements*. It attempts to fill the niche once occupied by the *Princeton Essays in International Finance*, a series that no longer exists.

There is a great deal of important work that takes place in international economics that is set out in highly theoretical and mathematical terms. This new Elements does not eschew this work but seeks a broader audience that includes academic economists and researchers, including those working in international organizations, such as the World Bank, the International Monetary Fund, and the Organization for Economic Cooperation and Development.

Cambridge Elements ≡

International Economics

Elements in the Series

Debt Sustainability: A Global Perspective
Ludger Schuknecht

The RMB in the Global Economy
Yin-Wong Cheung

Export Quality and Income Distribution
Rajat Acharyya and Shrimoyee Ganguly

The East Asian Electronics Sector: The Roles of Exchange Rates, Technology Transfer, and Global Value Chains
Willem Thorbecke

Virtual Trade in a Changing World: Comparative Advantage, Growth and Inequality
Sugata Marjit, Gouranga G. Das and Biswajit Mandal

International Investment Income
Joseph P. Joyce

How the Brady Plan Delivered on Debt Relief: Lessons and Implications
Neil Shenai and Marijn A. Bolhuis

A full series listing is available at: www.cambridge.org/CEIE

For EU product safety concerns, contact us at Calle de José Abascal, 56–1°, 28003 Madrid, Spain or eugpsr@cambridge.org.

www.ingramcontent.com/pod-product-compliance
Lightning Source LLC
LaVergne TN
LVHW011846060526
838200LV00054B/4184